Eating,

Sleeping,

and

Getting

Up

BROADWAY BOOKS
NEW YORK

# Eating, Sleeping, and Getting Up

How to Stop
the Daily Battles
with Your Child

## Carolyn Crowder, Ph.D.

BROADWAY

EATING, SLEEPING, AND GETTING UP. Copyright © 2002 by Carolyn
Crowder. All rights reserved. Printed in the United States of America.
No part of this book may be reproduced or transmitted in any form
or by any means, electronic or mechanical, including photocopying,
recording, or by any information storage and retrieval system,
without written permission from the publisher. For information,
address Broadway Books, a division of Random House, Inc.,
1540 Broadway, New York, NY 10036.

Broadway Books titles may be purchased for business or promotional
use or for special sales. For information, please write to: Special
Markets Department, Random House, Inc., 1540 Broadway,
New York, NY 10036.

BROADWAY BOOKS and its logo, a letter B bisected on the diagonal, are
trademarks of Broadway Books, a division of Random House, Inc.

Visit our website at www.broadwaybooks.com

Library of Congress Cataloging-in-Publication Data
Crowder, Carolyn Zoe.
 Eating, sleeping, and getting up: how to stop the daily battles with
 your child / Carolyn Crowder.— 1st ed.
  p.  cm.
 Includes index.
  1. Child rearing.  2. Discipline of children.  3. Respect for
 persons.  4. Responsibility.  I. Title.

HQ769 .C953 2002
649'.1—dc21

                                                    2001037467

FIRST EDITION

ISBN 0-7679-0777-9

10  9  8  7  6  5  4  3  2  1

*Designed by Jennifer Ann Daddio*

# Acknowledgments

I would first like to acknowledge Pat Skinner for her contribution to the writing of this book. She has the gift. She writes quickly and very well and I could not have completed this task without her. Her friendship, good common sense, and innate understanding of the concept of respect have helped me improve all my ways.

I want to thank my agent, Alice Martell, for her hard work on my behalf. Her support of this book has been an encouragement to me throughout the whole process.

Many thanks are also due Eva Dreikurs Ferguson who granted me permission to use Rudolf Dreikurs' quotes in this book. These insightful short statements were taken from her father's many books, which are listed in the Sources section at the end, and from her recently published pamphlet titled *Dreikurs Sayings*.

I also want to acknowledge my wonderful teacher and friend, Dr. Oscar Christensen, who has taught me so much about working with parents and children. Quotes of his that are used in this book were taken from twenty years of hearing him lecture and discuss Adlerian principles. He has changed the world for those he has reached—both his students and his clients.

I am indebted to the legacy that descends from Alfred Adler, through Rudolf Dreikurs, to Oscar Christensen. All three spent their lives working to improve relationships in families by teaching parents what the concept of respect really means in raising children.

*"I know of no more encouraging fact than the unquestionable ability of man to elevate his life by a conscious endeavor. To affect the quality of the day, that is the highest of arts."*

— HENRY DAVID THOREAU

# Contents

# Introduction

- Do your children cause trouble at mealtimes by refusing to eat, fighting at the table, or demanding something else?
- Do they use delay tactics to avoid going to bed, taking baths, or putting on their pajamas?
- Is it impossible to get them up in the morning? Once up, do they turn on the television set or video games and become immersed?
- Are you at a loss as to how to bring about any change in your negative interactions with them?

This book provides practical ways for you to respond effectively when faced with rudeness, lack of cooperation, and power struggles over the necessary daily tasks of eating, sleeping, and getting up in the mornings. More important, in these pages you will find an overall approach to raising children who are responsible and empathic toward others.

Techniques by themselves are not enough to bring about change over the long term in these common problem areas. Parents need to begin to think differently about their roles in relation to their offspring.

Modern-day parents, because they are often overwhelmed, have adopted low expectations for their children's behaviors. These parents have come to accept their children's misbehaviors as facts of life. They have become convinced that their children are not capable of learning to behave. When this happens, parents feel defeated and decide to give up expecting anything better from their kids.

While this position of "giving up" is understandable, it is the worst thing parents can do to their children. However, the methods that most adults have tried when it comes to raising their children, either attempting to overpower their children or catering to them, do not work, and parents do not understand why.

They simply cannot think of anything else to do. They throw up their hands in frustration and make wild statements they do not mean. For example, when children misbehave while eating in a restaurant or as guests at a neighbor's house, parents may end up shouting that "we will never take you children out in public again." These parents seem to be willing to tolerate rudeness and misbehavior inside the home, but they attempt to draw the line when they are embarrassed in front of others.

It is confusing to parents that these same children who embarrassed them at a function last night will turn around and behave well in their absence. They are often shocked when a neighbor or teacher tells them what a cooperative child they have and what a pleasure that child is to have around. While parents are happy and relieved that their children obviously know how to behave, they are resentful (and rightly so) that they, the parents, do not qualify for the same good treatment.

How much better it would be for all concerned if parents and children enjoyed each other as much as they seem to enjoy the company of others. That in itself is a worthy goal, and that is what can be achieved by adopting the attitudes and techniques suggested here.

What this book offers is a coherent, well-founded approach for parents to use in raising children. Most parents are in a reactive mode when misbehavior occurs. They have no plan, and so they simply react, usually inconsistently, to bad behavior. Parents become punitive or arbitrary or bribery-oriented just to try to get hold of the situation.

And, in addition to low expectations, many parents are driven not just by lack of faith in their children, but also by fear. These days, many parents are either afraid of what their children will become or they are so afraid of their children's power in the household that they turn a blind eye and just hope things will get better.

Fear clouds the issue for parents so that they routinely do one of two things when their children misbehave. They blow a situation completely out of proportion and become punitive toward the child, or they make excuses for bad behavior and do not deal with it at all. Neither method is effective. At their base, both of these approaches are disrespectful because they do not teach, nor do they allow the child to take responsibility for his actions.

Problems arise when parents go on "automatic pilot," not really thinking philosophically about their children and how they should be raised, but responding from a set of old and sometimes unconscious beliefs gleaned from many different sources. People form their parenting patterns based on such things as their own parents' modes of discipline (or lack thereof), popular child-rearing fads of the moment, or their experiences as children.

Grown-ups typically take a position either "for" or "in opposition to" what their own parents did and then find themselves falling back on the worst examples of parental responses when their backs are against the wall. They do or say things that they have vowed from childhood they will never do or say!

This book will provide you with new responses that will help with discipline in the best sense of the word, that is, to teach children as opposed to punishing them or catering to them. You will learn a parenting philosophy that will change your relationship with your children and that is also applicable in every area of your life. It is a philosophy based on mutual respect, cooperation, contribution, taking responsibility for yourself and your behaviors (and allowing your children to do so, as well), and having expectations that members of your family can learn to treat each other better.

Do any of the following statements describe the beliefs you currently hold about your children?

- Parents should be the bosses.
- Parents ought to be able to control their children because they are bigger, stronger, and know more.

- Sometimes spanking, yelling, and threatening are the only techniques that get immediate results.
- It is all right for parents to fall back on a bribery and reward system to get children to behave properly (i.e., "If you stop crying while we're in the restaurant, I will buy you a cookie on the way out"). The end justifies the means.
- Using threats of punishment is a good way to let children know you are the boss. They will think about what is coming and behave better to avoid the punishment.
- Parents do not actually have to follow through with appropriate discipline for misbehavior. Talking is enough.
- Parents should not have high expectations for how well their children can behave. After all, they are only children.
- Parents can settle for less when it comes to children's behavior at home. If parents can just get children to behave in public, they can let up in private. Nobody is as good at home as they are in public.
- Being a good parent means protecting children so they do not have to face the consequences of their actions. They are too young to be held responsible.
- Children should not have to contribute to the family and take on obligations such as chores. After all, they are only children for so long.
- Parents do not need to worry about being respectful in the way they talk to their children. Establishing power and control is more important.
- Children seldom show respect for their parents. All children are rebellious and at odds with adults.
- Good parents continually lecture, remind, coax, nag, reprimand, and criticize children about what they are doing wrong. This is how children learn.

- Parents will be successful at childrearing if they are permissive and indulge their children. Kids will like you, and, therefore, they will want to behave.
- The best way to raise children is by instilling fear of their parents. That will make them behave.

You may have found yourself nodding your head in agreement with these statements. You may not have realized that you even think these things. But not one of these beliefs helps you raise children who are thoughtful of others or who are responsible for themselves and their actions.

In fact, these beliefs hinder your ability to teach your children how to behave and do not model good behavior that you want them to adopt for themselves. It is possible that you are being held back by many of these beliefs, and that, in fact, giving up even a few of them will free you to have very different relationships with your children.

Furthermore, if you are serious about giving up some of these beliefs and readjusting the way you think about your methods of discipline, you will find that you are able to change. In your role as a parent and the leader in your family, you will take charge of your part in the negative dynamics that may be wreaking havoc in your own family.

Changing these dynamics is your job, not your children's. The job of restructuring the way family members relate and respond to one another is your responsibility. Parents need to look for their children's input and cooperation, but you are the leader here.

This book will teach you how to establish a better atmosphere around the specific tasks of eating, sleeping, and getting up. The methods taught for handling these three arenas can be applied across the board for all other misbehaviors, as well.

## Approaches to Parenting

Raising children is the most difficult, demanding, and important job you will ever face. It is so important to us as a society, in fact, that a cottage industry has grown up around techniques for parenting. Over the years, you may have watched fads come and go, everything from "you will do it because I say so" to the kind of permissiveness that allows toddlers to rule the roost. You may even have tried some of these "flavors of the month" yourself. But they haven't worked, have they? At least, they have not produced good, long-term results.

Many of the approaches to parenting that are bandied about these days are set up to fail because they do little more than offer parents a "quick fix." "If you do *A,* your child will behave like *B.*" It goes something like this: "If you pay your child an allowance to do household chores, you will never have to nag the child again and all the chores will get done because the child wants the money." It sounds good to you since you have not attempted this approach before, so you try it.

Yet, when you set up this scheme with your child, you find that it really only works for a short period of time. Inevitably, the day comes when the allowance does not motivate the child and the chores are not done. Now you must nag or threaten to withhold the allowance unless the child does what you have asked. The quick fix didn't work, and, worse, the lesson your child learned is that he is expected to contribute to the family only when he is paid to do so.

## Respectful Parenting

This book does not offer a quick fix, although the approach offered here often begins to work very quickly. This book delineates a few simple yet sound principles that are based on common sense and that reflect an attitude about life that is good for both parents and their children. It is an attitude and an approach to life defined by mutual respect, firm yet kind parental leadership, and a commitment to teaching children how to participate in the give and take of living with others.

At its foundation is a basic understanding about establishing real respect (self-respect and respect for others) so that children know and will want to do what is expected of them as members of the family.

This philosophy of human relationships is rooted in theories of behavior developed by Alfred Adler (1870–1937) and his follower, Rudolf Dreikurs (1897–1972). Adler disagreed with Freud's belief in the biological or sexual basis for behavior. His approach was built around viewing behavior in its *social* context. Adler believed the infant impacted his environment as much as it impacted him. He was interested in the factors of birth order and family atmosphere.

Dreikurs took Adler's philosophy of psychology and created a practical parenting approach that has proved useful to many parents and teachers over the years. He trained professionals and parents in America and across the world throughout his lifetime. One of his most influential students, Dr. Oscar Christensen, was my mentor.

These men believed that a parent's response to a child's behavior served either to encourage or discourage that behavior. As Dreikurs says, "We are constantly influencing each other positively or negatively." Parents influence children, and, from the moment they are born, children influence their parents.

These parent educators also believed that children thrive within families where they are valued for their contributions and are expected to behave in positive ways. This common sense, practical, "Adlerian" approach is the foundation for everything offered in the pages that follow.

Adler and Dreikurs believed that children (like all of us) are looking for ways to belong and feel significant in the social world. Children flail about when young, trying "a little of this and a little of that" types of behavior to see what kind of response they get. If children are denied avenues of belonging that are positive in nature (such as helping others, being responsible, cooperating) they will eventually hit upon behaviors that bring a negative response from mom and dad.

At times, parents unwittingly stifle their children's attempts to find positive ways of belonging because they hold certain beliefs and attitudes about children, which they then act on. For example, your three-year-old wants to help you cook a meal, and when you answer, "No, you are not old enough yet," you discourage the child's natural desire to help, depriving him of belonging through contribution.

In addition, you have given the child a negative message about wanting to cooperate within the family and shown little faith that the child can learn to do things. Something you have said, almost without thinking, can be in reality a confusing and troubling message to a young child who is looking for ways to help, to emulate you, and to do the things "big people" do.

Think about the number of times parents discourage their children between the ages of, say, two and five years old. Hundreds of these discouraging, stifling messages coming from mom and dad will produce a six-year-old who has a poor attitude about doing anything he is asked to do.

It is essential, though occasionally inconvenient, to take the time to let your child, no matter how young, learn how to do things and help you. Your patience and care will be rewarded in the future, and that is how you have to look at this time spent being "inconvenienced" by training your children.

When positive avenues are blocked by parents who send these kinds of discouraging messages, children look for other ways to gain a place of significance and get their parents' attention. The negative reactions (annoyance, anger, hurt) children receive in response to misbehavior serve to make them feel significant and important, and they will then repeat the behaviors. They will come to believe that "I am only significant when I am bossing you or getting even." They will then repeat those behaviors that bring them these feelings of power.

This book begins with a quote that is very apt, and it is the first thing parents must consider if you are truly interested in understanding and changing the atmosphere at home. You must stop doing what you are currently doing. That, in and of itself, will bring about change. As Rudolf Dreikurs says, "Merely not doing the wrong thing is not enough, but it helps."

You may begin by some simple experimentation with a few of your own behaviors. If you lecture and nag, be quiet. If you scream, threaten, or spank, try making simple, calm statements without any physical accompaniment. If you are tired of doing all the work around the house, go on a polite "strike" and sit down without talking about it. Just do it and note the responses of your children.

It is extremely important as you begin this work to observe the reactions your children have to your new behaviors. You need to see how dramatic being quiet is when you have formerly been loud. Note the effect that the simple change in your behavior has on your children and on the family atmosphere (not to mention on your stress level). And do not be dismayed if the changes you see at first are small.

Parents often criticize their children's efforts in the right direction because the outcome is not exactly what they want. Do not be this kind of discouraging parent. Learn to build on even small successes.

## The Daily Grind

This book guides you through three specific areas of daily family conflict: eating, sleeping, and getting up. These routine tasks represent the ideal training grounds for parents to begin to adopt new attitudes and techniques. As adults change their behaviors, they thereby influence their children to change, as well.

If you employ these principles as you work with your children throughout the "daily grind," you will see almost immediate improvement in their behavior.

A wonderful side benefit of employing this approach is that you are more in control of your emotions and responses. Your stress level will go way down when you are no longer getting upset, angry, resentful, hurt, or frustrated by your children's behavior.

Think about the dynamics of your day this way: Everyone must eat, sleep, and get out of bed each morning. Within every family, there is a whirlwind of activity. Mom and dad must get to work on time and children have to go to school or day care. It seems so simple. If everyone does what must be done, things can run smoothly.

The reality is that most families are locked in combat around these three times of the day. Dreikurs notes that, "Our homes and our schools are filled with acts of mutual warfare." Because no alternative plan of action has been put into place, parents and children begin and end their days with battles for power and control. This cycle is exhausting, demoralizing, and never ending. Parents find themselves arguing, reminding, coaxing, or bribing in order to get their children to complete the simplest of tasks.

Children who misuse their power to define their roles in the family utilize these times of stress to assert that they are the bosses and the parents cannot "make them" do anything. When the children refuse to do what they are supposed to do, parents find themselves screaming louder, nagging longer, and threatening endless punishments that they and the children both know will never be forthcoming.

This is the traumatic cycle that so many parents and children engage in as they try to accomplish the simplest requirements of daily living. Nothing seems to work. Why? Because people have not educated themselves in very simple concepts that will help them navigate through these power struggles.

Let's take a look at a common scenario you may recognize. After another morning battle to get everybody up, dressed, fed, and out the door on time, mom puts in a full day at work, stops at the grocery store to pick up something for dinner, and then cooks dinner.

*When dinner is ready, mom sets the table, and calls for her three children to come eat. Dad is working late, which he often does, to avoid the evening conflicts and chaos. Her children drift in, one by one. The oldest, a twelve-year-old daughter, makes a face at the plate of food and carries it off to her room. The nine-year-old son whines that he does not like what he sees and demands that mother cook something else for him. Soon the six-year-old son enters and declares that he is watching his favorite television program and dinner will have to wait.*

*Mom makes sarcastic and angry remarks to each of her children in turn, and their responses include arguments, eye rolling, and whining as, one by one, they turn their backs on her and leave the dining area. Is it any wonder she feels resentful and unappreciated? She wishes her husband were there to help her. She wishes she had come up with the excuse of working late as a way to avoid all of this rude behavior and conflict.*

*Anger and resentment are soon replaced by dread, however, as mom eats alone and then begins to clean up the kitchen. She is already anticipating the struggle yet to come, as she wrangles the children through baths and bedtimes. By the time she finds a few minutes to spend with her husband, she will be too angry and resentful to talk and relax with him, so she can probably count on adding another unproductive and unpleasant bit of conflict to her day.*

*She will finish this stress-filled and fatiguing day and, presto!, it is time to wake up again and begin another round of hassles to get everybody fed, dressed, and out the door.*

*Each day is a repeat of the day before. Neither of these parents knows what to do. They have tried lecturing, inducing guilt, spanking, and bribing. Now they simply accept the conflict as inevitable and either contribute to it or avoid it altogether.*

*The chaos is affecting their marriage, not to mention the damage it is doing to the family unit. They love each other and their children, but life is so difficult when it is lived this way every day.*

It is no wonder family stress is escalating when parents and children are locked in combat over the daily activities of living. But, rather than accepting this way of life as "the way it is," parents must begin to see that these activities do not have to be battlegrounds. There is another way to do things, and you, the parent, can introduce beneficial changes rather than just giving up and accepting a painful and disheartening routine of chaos and power struggles.

It all begins with you, and, for that reason, this book focuses on helping parents change their reactions to their children's misbehavior, rather than trying to change their children. People who have used these techniques find that when parents change their responses, kids will soon give up their misbehaviors. Typically, however, most parents have not considered the ideas in this book, and so they react to their children in ways that only escalate the battles.

These are parents who have not given much thought to the

way they now do things. They have not considered that they may be contributing to their child's misbehaviors. Many of them are astonished when they learn that controlling their own responses instead of trying to control their children brings an end to their cycle of fighting over eating, sleeping, and getting up.

It is a simple concept, but it is also one that takes commitment and practice on the part of parents. There is a lot of work to be done before this plan can be implemented. It is essential that you read through this book and then give all the ideas and techniques a great deal of thought. You must be fully committed to this approach before you begin or you may make things worse instead of better.

There are new attitudes and behaviors for you to adopt, and you must make up your mind that you will be consistent and follow through. If you implement a consequence and later cave in, you have only taught the child that it will take longer to wear you down. You will have essentially upped the ante.

This system is not easy, and it requires effort on your part. The rewards are great, but the work is hard. The concepts are simple, but they are not easy to put into action. Changing your responses so that you are interacting differently with your children does not come naturally. It is learned behavior, but over time, your new responses will become as natural to you as the yelling and bribing you do now.

## Breaking the Cycle

It is paradoxical but true that many parents become comfortable with discomfort. It is not easy to break cycles of behavior that have become habitual. Many parents have become used to nagging or punishing as a means of getting their children to complete the simple tasks of getting through each day.

What are these parents to do? Where can they go for answers to help them bring peace, loving kindness, and cooperation to the family? They certainly do not have time to read much of the information that is available out there, let alone try to put all the techniques into practice. That is why a book such as this can really help. The use of concise steps and strategies presented here can produce change in your children very quickly.

Of these steps and strategies, the two most important are:

- allowing children to experience consequences for misbehaviors
- allowing them to find positive ways of belonging in the family through contribution and thoughtfulness

## Consequences

When you do not respond in your typical way of yelling, threatening, punishing, or bribing, you probably think that you have done nothing and the child has gotten away with bad behavior. To fully understand the idea of enacting consequences when your children misbehave, you must accept that the lack of your typical response does not mean that nothing has happened.

As Dreikurs says, "By doing nothing in a power contest, you defeat the child's power." This is not to say that you should ignore your child's bad behavior. He is suggesting that your action should be based on a plan that involves logical consequences,

not the typical punishment or bribery techniques you have relied on in the past.

When you implement logical consequences, the child must
focus on his own behavior and what has resulted from his actions instead of focusing on you and your anger. If you yell at
him or threaten to punish him, both of you get caught up in the
conflict and soon lose sight of the real issue at hand, his misbehavior.

If, however, you change that response and take action with
very few or no words, and, for example, you react to your child's
misbehavior by calmly leaving a public place, the child is forced
to acknowledge that his misbehavior comes with a consequence.
The child knows you will most likely leave other places in the
future if he chooses to continue to misbehave. This is a real
learning experience for the child, whereas, engaging as one half
of the power struggle teaches nothing.

Instead of your anger and the escalating conflict being at the
center of things, the focus is on the child, where it should be.
What if, in retaliation, the child says, "That's okay. I didn't
want to be here anyway." You may feel defeated, thinking that
you have had no effect on him when you implemented the consequence of leaving.

But that is how a powerful child wants you to feel. With
these words, he is still trying to pull you back into the power
struggle. It would be typical to respond, "Well, I certainly will
not bring you again!" Now, you see, you are off and running.
His bid for power worked.

The truth of the matter is that it is more helpful if you
believe in what you are doing and adopt the attitude that
your children want to be with you. You are the parents, and,

therefore, the most important people in your children's lives. Whether they are three, thirteen, or twenty-three, your children want you.

A child who says, "I don't care. I didn't want to be here anyway," is using a technique to make you feel defeated in your use of the consequence of leaving. Since you didn't fuss and carry on, as he is used to, he is now trying to provoke the familiar game that has become your routine together. His statement is not genuine, and it should not be taken personally.

This child is trying to get the upper hand and manipulate you into the old struggle where he gets to feel important and powerful (for all the wrong reasons). It is a game of "tit for tat." But remember that this kind of game cannot be played alone. If you do not engage, it cannot go on. Furthermore, you keep the child from diverting both you and him from the consequence.

No matter what the child says about not caring about your leaving, the new pattern is very clear to him. The child misbehaves. You leave. No matter how he tries to manipulate the situation by bravado, he is experiencing fully the consequence of his misbehavior. Trust the fact that your children want to do what is right. As Dreikurs says, "Every child knows what he should do, but that does not mean that he will do it."

If this is the case, then why do children choose not to do the right thing? Quite simply, the child is used to the old routine that has probably been in place for quite some time. In the past, he has engaged in gaining belonging and significance through power, which has worked for him because of the way you have responded.

Now, as you begin to change things, you need to trust that your child knows what is right and wants to do it, regardless of past or current behavior. Assume that next time he will do the right thing because you have taught him that his misbehavior has consequences, which you will allow him to experience.

You may have to repeat this pattern several times for it to take hold, but it will take hold. Your consistency and firmness are the keys to creating new ways for you and your children to respond to each other. This is the time to have faith that progress is being made and will become evident soon.

Note small changes and continue on. Take encouragement from the times your children begin to make even slight changes in their behavior. Focus on making changes in yourself first. Some of these new responses and attitudes will get immediate results, and some may take a little longer. Hang in there!

## Contribution

Adler wrote, "Every human being strives for significance; but people always make mistakes if they do not see that their whole significance must consist in their contribution to the lives of others." Adler recognized the great importance of finding meaning in life through giving to and helping others.

This is the other extremely important concept to understand philosophically as you begin to implement these new techniques and attitudes. The idea of contribution is one that parents must adopt if they are to change the dynamics within their families. Children can and should contribute to the family in meaningful ways.

It is a grave mistake to think your children do not want to assume chores, help out with family routines, and take part in the daily maintenance of the household. Children need to contribute, just as adults do, in order to feel important and useful to those they love.

The wise parents who accept this about their children and encourage them to be fully contributing family members do their children another service, as well. Adler believed that children are born with a natural desire to acquire skills and be helpful.

Those who are allowed to take their rightful place in the family through contribution learn valuable life skills that give them self-confidence and make them feel productive and active. They learn the value of the positive consequences of belonging in cooperative, helpful ways. They no longer need to gain negative attention or selfish power to feel important in the family. And they gain in positive ways by learning about caring for others and assuming social responsibility, which are both important to their adult futures. As Dr. Oscar Christensen says, every child should feel, "This family would fall apart without me!"

This book's emphasis on contribution should not be taken lightly. It is the cornerstone of effective parenting. Remember, when children are not allowed to be part of the family through the avenue of contribution, they will turn to misbehavior to gain power, feel important, and belong.

Contribution entails not just doing chores, but also thinking of others, pitching in when a family member needs support, sharing, making life easier for others, and just generally doing what is expected because it needs to be done. These are all examples of a spirit of contribution that can become part of your family's routine just as the spirit of conflict is now.

Remember when your children were toddlers? Remember how much they wanted to help and learn how to do things? Where did that go? Well, it disappeared into power struggles and attention-getting misbehaviors because you most likely did not allow or encourage the child to help. Maybe you thought you should do everything yourself. Maybe you are a perfectionist who couldn't stand to see a toddler attempt to wash dishes.

Maybe you were too tired to teach them and it was just easier to do it yourself. You unthinkingly thwarted the child's attempt to belong in positive ways. But it is not too late to begin again. It is just a little more difficult because now your children are a bit older and are used to the patterns you have established with them.

It is helpful to keep in mind Rudolf Dreikurs' assertion, "The greatest stimulation for the development of the child is exposing him to experiences which seem to be beyond his reach but are not."

Use the many suggestions and ideas you will find here to begin to change your family dynamics. And do not stop there. Come up with some ideas of your own. You may even ask your children (and probably should) what they believe should happen the next time that they choose to ignore their responsibilities. Let them think up some consequences on their own. This is a great learning opportunity. You will learn what your children think, and they will learn that you value their opinions in a positive way. Also, you will have a meaningful list of consequences to enact should that become necessary.

## This Chapter in a Nutshell

This book addresses just three basic problems, but they are problems shared by almost all parents. What is more, these difficulties are rooted in the same ineffective approaches that keep parents stuck in the never-ending cycle of escalating skirmishes and open warfare that too many families are willing to accept as "just the way things have to be."

- Eating, sleeping, and getting up are the three areas of daily conflict fueled by common mistakes that nearly all parents make at some time or another.
- Unfortunately, many parents hold tight to certain beliefs and behaviors that create an unstable foundation. The likelihood for strife within a family is thereby increased.

If you are busy fighting and punishing while your children are using all their time for sulking, misbehaving, and getting revenge, there is no enjoyment, no laughter, and no sharing for anybody. Your children can come to be a pleasure and a joy in your life as they decide to be well-behaved, responsible youngsters. Too often parents forget that they can laugh, tease, hug, and play with their children. They can share those special bits of wisdom and unique perspectives that only children can bring to us.

Begin with small steps. Take stock of yourself. What kind of parent are you? What are you teaching your children? What kind of parents were your own mother and father? What didn't work then that you are still trying to use now? Becoming a better parent is a journey that begins with self-knowledge.

As an adult receptive to change and willing to examine and discard the myths and misconceptions you have relied on in relation to your children, you can become a better and more relaxed parent. You can learn:

- simple, common sense principles that often get results quickly
- a new plan of action with which to respond to your children's misbehavior
- a parenting philosophy that builds strong self-concepts in children and strong, loving relationships within the family

There is no better time than right now to institute the positive changes your family needs. Peace, harmony, and cooperation within the family are not just unrealistic illusions. They are practical, achievable goals, and you have a right to enjoy them. So roll up your sleeves, and let's get started. There are better days ahead.

# 1.

# Why Children Misbehave and What You Can Do About It

*"Discouragement is at the root of all misbehavior."*

—RUDOLF DREIKURS

Understanding why your children misbehave is not as difficult and daunting as it may first seem. Perhaps because we are living in a complicated world we are constantly looking for complicated answers, especially when it comes to examining human behavior. Yet Adler and Dreikurs knew that misbehaviors in children ought to be approached at the simplest level.

Your children misbehave because they have become discouraged about finding a positive place of significance within the family. Each child needs to feel he or she is an important and useful member of the family unit. Because this desire for significance is so important, children work to achieve this goal through either negative or positive means.

Think of your family as a sports team. Parents are the coaches, and each child is a supporting member of the team. What happens when a team member does not perform at a productive level? The team does not function as well as it might, just as your family fails to perform when each member is not helping to maintain it in productive and positive ways.

Children want to be important members of their family's team. They are looking to the "coaches" to tell them how to do that. Sadly, the coaches are falling down on the job because they are failing to provide the guidance children need to understand what is expected of them and how they must behave and perform if the family is to function smoothly and happily.

When parents do not behave like leaders, children become insecure within their small worlds. If they can boss mom and dad around, then whom will they look to for guidance and protection? Children know they are not capable of assuming the leadership role in the family. It makes them feel vulnerable and insecure when they do not have parents who will set limits and teach them how to behave.

Parents who are truly good leaders or, using our sports metaphor, good coaches, serve as models of positive behavior for their children. They set the standard by which the family will behave, not by brute strength or superior size, but by cooperation, contribution, and respect for all members of the family. These parents realize that allowing children to be useful is an antidote to all kinds of misbehavior.

It is also important to note that these parents are doing a service to the larger society at the same time they are helping their own families. They are teaching life principles that will affect other aspects of their children's lives as they marry, work, and raise children of their own.

They also know that it is up to parents to teach children what the positive behaviors should be and then to believe that their children are capable and responsible enough to rise to the occasion. When parents do not teach children how to behave, children learn to become "important" through negative means. Bad behavior gets your attention, doesn't it? Makes you angry? Hurts your feelings? Makes you feel like giving up?

Quite simply, children use misbehaviors to create for themselves a place of importance through power in relation to others. These traits do not go away by themselves. Children who successfully gain attention through power and negative behaviors will become more and more tyrannical as they get older. And these children will become more and more discouraged about belonging in any other way.

Once you accept this simple concept of "needing to feel important" as the foundation of your children's misbehavior, you are ready to do something about it. This idea should be foremost in your mind as you begin teaching your children to be courageous in facing the tasks of living with others in the community of the family, school, church, and larger society.

Children who work against others in their striving to feel important really do not feel capable of participating in respectful relationships. All they know is power and the struggle to dominate and control others. They have not learned about cooperation and contribution and the good feelings that come from these behaviors.

Your child is much more than his misbehavior, yet, as parents, you may find it much easier to see the child only in terms of what he does wrong. This is something you must work to overcome. You might begin by making a mental list of your children's good attributes to have ready for those times when you become discouraged and focus too intently on the misbehaviors.

If you take the ideas in this book to heart, you will change the way you do things and become more respectful of your children. As you teach them to become responsible members of the family, you will see the importance of relishing and encouraging your children's good behavior, not just dealing with the bad.

Many parents are surprised to learn that children blossom with sometimes just a few words of acknowledgment that they have done the right thing. In fact, rewarding them with toys, candy, and privileges is unnecessary and downright insulting to the child who is actually eager to help.

## Learning New Parental Responses

Your parental responses to misbehavior often serve to aggravate and promote continued acting out by your children. This is another important idea that you must accept and learn from if you are to successfully change the dynamics within your family. The two most common responses parents use are the autocratic ("I am the boss") or the indulgent ("permissive pal"). Neither of these responses teaches children how to behave. You must see yourself as a teacher and guide who is there to share wisdom and implement constructive discipline so that children may learn. They need your leadership as much as they need your love.

It is a misconception to think that one can supplant the other. Children learn how to behave from the actions modeled by their parents, as well as by dealing with the consequences of their own behaviors. Consistent parental discipline actively shows children the relationship between behavior and consequences.

Let's look at an example of how this all plays out by comparing different parental responses to a bedtime situation:

*Five-year-old Tiffany is finally in bed after what seems like hours of dawdling. She whined and complained when told it was bath time. Mom also had to tell her over and over again to brush her teeth and put on her pajamas. Then Tiffany had to have a drink of water, followed by another trip to the bathroom. After that, it was story time. When one story was finished, the child begged for another.*

*When mom finally said no and turned off the light, the child began to scream and cry. Mom left the room, but what now? She can hear Tiffany screaming and crying and fears she will work herself up into a full-blown tantrum.*

*A mom who is the "boss" will return to the room and threaten Tiffany with punishment such as a spanking or withdrawal of the privilege of riding her bike the next day. She will probably do this several times before Tiffany finally falls asleep.*

*A mom who is the "permissive pal" feels sorry for the child and will return to the room many times to cajole or bribe her with treats. She will pamper and pet the crying child and perhaps read her several more stories or bring her more water or snacks.*

*However, a respectful, responsible mother will let the child scream and cry without any response at all. This mother knows that she has to let the child experience the consequences of her own behavior. The child may continue to cry and scream, but mom can and should choose not to respond because she understands the child is not really in distress.*

*The wailing is a technique to gain power and attention and keep mom involved. She has other things to do, and the child needs to learn to appreciate that.*

*Otherwise, the child learns "it is all about me, and I only count when mom is serving me." This child learns that it is okay to disrupt her mother's time and create conflict as long as she gets the attention she wants.*

*An awareness of others (even moms!) as people who have needs of their own is not taught by a parent who is the "boss" or the "permissive pal." However, a respectful mother teaches her child that she is a person separate from her child and that she has things she must do. The child learns to help mom by going to bed and sleeping when it is time to do so.*

*Is it cruel to let a child scream and cry because she does not want to go to bed and get to sleep? Let's consider this. From the "boss" mother, Tiffany learns that "might makes right." From the "permissive pal" mother, the child learns that screaming and crying work wonders, and she will be rewarded with mom's attention no matter how bad her behavior becomes.*

*From the respectful, responsible mother, however, Tiffany learns that her misbehavior gets her nowhere, and she soon stops it on her own. It may take a couple of nights for Tiffany to learn this valuable lesson, but what are a*

*couple of nights compared to a possible lifetime of scream-*
*ing and abusing others to get what she wants?*

This example brings up another important point that is also so simple that we often overlook it. The truth is that children will never respect parents who do not respect themselves. Parents need to understand how their own behavior can reflect a basic disrespect of themselves and their roles within the family.

In the example with Tiffany, the "permissive pal" mom is a doormat who sacrifices her own peace of mind and relaxation in order to respond to her child's tantrums and misbehaviors. Mother has a right to quiet time at the end of the day. She has a right to expect that her child will perform the necessary activities to get ready for bed, and that she will go to sleep on time and in a helpful manner.

Instead, this mother feels that she must cater to a spoiled child who will come to believe that "I am the center of the universe." Since the rest of the world will never treat her this way, this mother is actually doing a disservice to her child. But, just as important, she is also failing to respect herself and her own needs when she martyrs herself this way.

The "boss" mom is also doing a disservice, for she is failing to act and speak respectfully to her child. This is an essential component of effective parenting. Parents must respect their children, as well as themselves. An atmosphere of respect precludes participating in power struggles.

When the "boss" mom screams back and threatens Tiffany with dire punishments, all she does is give the child license to retaliate with more misbehavior until the situation escalates to unbearable levels. For a child to learn to respect others, the parent must treat the child respectfully and demonstrate self-

respect (no doormats or tyrants allowed!). It is essential to remember at all times that your responses carry far more weight
than just the reaction of the moment.

Your responses are road maps to adult behavior, and your
children look at what you do as the model for what they should
do (and most likely will do in the future). This is quite a bur-
den for parents to bear. Our behavior is not just ours. It influences our children, as well.

Parents must take a cold, hard look at themselves if they
wish their children's behaviors to improve. Are you a "permissive pal" or the "boss" with your own children? Take this brief
quiz to clarify what kind of parent you are.

Just circle the letter of the answer that most appropriately de-
scribes how you would respond to the child's behavior in each instance. Be honest with yourself as you assess what you would do.

## PARENT SELF-ASSESSMENT QUIZ

1. It is past bedtime, but six-year-old Bobby tells his parents
   he does not want to go to bed because he does not like to
   be in his room alone in the dark. Mom takes Bobby to the
   bedroom and tucks him in. Bobby gets up several times
   crying and complaining and telling mom and dad he is
   afraid and he cannot sleep. If you are Bobby's parent, you:

   a. Escort the child to his room and make a big display of
      opening up the closet, looking under the bed, chasing
      away "monsters," and plugging in a night-light. After
      Bobby is tucked in, you stay for a bit and soothe his
      fears. When he gets out of bed repeatedly, crying each

time, you take him back to his room and go through the whole procedure of chasing away scary creatures. Bobby finally settles down for the night after you tell him that if he'll stay in bed and go to sleep you will take him shopping for a toy on Saturday.

b. You put your foot down and let Bobby know that is is past his bedtime and that he must go to sleep *now*. He gets up crying, and you take him back to bed telling him that next time he gets up he'll get a spanking. Once he's back in bed, you leave the room after telling Bobby that if he does not settle down right now, you will take away his bicycle for a month.

c. You acknowledge that Bobby is afraid of the dark and tell him that you will put the night-light on for him. You read him one story and tuck him in for the night. When he gets up crying, you do not respond to his misbehavior other than to return him to his room. You do not tell him he must go back to bed or talk to him at all. He knows. Then you go on about your evening's activities.

2. Eight-year-old twins Sammy and Suzy come to the dinner table and refuse to eat what their mother and father have prepared. Sammy pushes his food around on the plate and tells mom and dad that he's not hungry. Then he asks if he can go back and watch his television program instead of sitting at the table. Suzy says she is very hungry, but she does not want to eat any vegetables, and she does not like mother's meatloaf. She wants tacos and a soft drink for dinner. Confronted with this behavior at the table, you:

a. Tell Sammy and Suzy you are sick and tired of having to call them over and over again to come to dinner. You say you do not know when you have run into two more ungrateful children and that after a hard day's work you didn't feel like making dinner anyway. You tell the two of them that if they do not eat every bite of food that is on their plates you will send them to their rooms and that they will not be allowed to play with their friends after school for a month.

b. You simply state that they need to eat now because the next meal will be breakfast. You ignore their complaints and do not respond. You then finish your own dinner, clear the table, and put the remaining food away regardless of whether the children have eaten or not.

c. You become worried that your children will get sick if they do not eat. You leave your own dinner on the table to prepare tacos for Suzy. You go to the family room where Sammy is watching television and tell him he has to eat something or he'll get sick. You ask him what he wants to eat, and when he tells you he wants a peanut butter and jelly sandwich and some cookies, you bring those to him on a tray so he can eat while he's watching television. It is better that they eat something even if it means extra work for you.

3. Seven-year-old Briana cannot seem to wake up on time. She stays in bed even though mom calls her several times. When she finally gets up, she dawdles with her clothes and then pokes at her breakfast. Then she cannot find her

schoolwork and one of her favorite hair clips is missing.
She spends time looking for it, and will not finish getting
ready for school. If you are Briana's mother, you could:

a. Calmly and reasonably explain to Briana that you must
   leave the house at exactly 7:30 A.M. and that when that
   time comes you will be taking her to school, ready or
   not. Then do so.

b. You stop what you are doing and help Briana search for
   her hair clip. You know how important it is to her to
   wear that special clip, and you do not want her to think
   you do not care about how she looks when she goes to
   school. Then you spend time helping her find her
   schoolwork and getting it organized. This takes quite a
   bit of extra time. You must now rush through the rest
   of your own preparations for work, and everyone will
   be late getting where they are going. But at least Briana
   is happy.

c. You yell at Briana until she finally gets up. You are so
   frustrated by these mornings when nothing goes right
   that you snap at her when she cannot find her hair clip
   and demand that she use another one. You tell her if she
   does not get her act together you are going to make her
   go to bed every night at six o'clock until she can manage to get up on time.

If you have really tried to respond to these scenarios objec-
tively and evaluate your own parenting techniques honestly,
then the following answers will not come as any surprise to you.

Question 1:
    A = permissive pal (doormat)
    B = boss
    C = respectful, responsible parent

Question 2:
    A = boss
    B = respectful, responsible parent
    C = permissive pal (doormat)

Question 3:
    A = respectful, responsible parent
    B = permissive pal (doormat)
    C = boss

The most important thing to take from this brief test is not a sense of whether or not you are a good or bad parent, but whether you sometimes act as a "permissive pal," a "boss," or a respectful, responsible parent. You may find that at different times you bounce quickly between "boss" and "permissive pal." Many parents placate and coddle, but when that does not work and the child keeps pushing, they come down hard with punishments or threats.

The trick is to identify which kinds of responses are the most prevalent for you and then to seek ways to become a respectful, responsible parent all of the time. Consistency is the key to becoming a better parent.

Two of these modes of interacting with your children do not get the results you are after. Bosses, doormats, or combinations of the two are not effective as parenting approaches. Once you transform yourself, you will begin to see great changes in your children. When you stop ordering them around or lying down to let them walk on you, you begin to see the level of respect rise between you and your children.

Painful as it may be to confront your shortcomings as parents, it is essential for you to do so if you truly want to help your children learn to behave another way. You, as adults, must be the ones who take the initial responsibility to change the dynamics in your families and create an atmosphere of peace and cooperation at home.

At the same time, your goal as parents must be to raise independent, caring, and respectful children. You must "keep your eyes on the prize" and realize that all the work you are doing is for the common good of the family and the well-being of your children.

Congratulations on taking the first introspective step toward understanding your own behavior. In the next chapters, we will explore how your parental role affects your children in the arenas of eating, sleeping, and getting up, and we will discuss ways in which you can change your own behavior and create new models that will teach your children positive ways of being important within the family.

Now here is another brief exercise you can use to help you isolate your behavior and become more aware of when and how your "boss" or "permissive pal" parent comes out. Write out your responses to the following:

*The last time I prepared a meal at home, my child/children said*

_____

_____

_____

_____

*When this happened, I felt*

_____

_____

_____

_____

*I responded by*

_____

_____

_____

_____

*In this instance, I was a*     boss     permissive pal     respectful
                                                            parent

*When this happens again, I can*

_____

_____

_____

_____

_____

_____

Pick out some specific examples of times your children have misbehaved in the arenas of eating, sleeping, and getting up. Write out your responses to your child's negative behaviors when involved in these three daily battles.

By writing out your responses to a variety of situations, you will begin to see clear patterns of behavior emerging, patterns that you and your children repeat several times a day, patterns that can be changed. You will also begin to see how your responses to your children's words and behaviors help escalate the conflict or fuel the misbehaviors.

By writing about what you can do differently next time, you will be setting the stage for change. Remember that thought is the first step toward action. You must create in your own mind new scenes that you can play out the next time your children's misbehaviors occur.

There is no substitute for planning when it comes to accomplishing positive changes. "Winging it" does not work when you are setting up a disciplined and productive routine to replace chaotic patterns of conflict.

All the techniques you are going to learn for dealing with misbehaviors that arise out of eating, sleeping, and getting up can be used to address other problems that occur with your children. There is no magic formula for possessing and using this knowledge to promote positive change within your family. You need only two things, and they are the willingness to learn and change, and the commitment to follow through when things become difficult.

So, with open minds and willing hearts, let's tackle the formidable battlegrounds of eating, sleeping, and getting up.

## This Chapter in a Nutshell

- A parent's first duty is to be a teacher and guide who shows children how to be positive, productive, respectful members of the family and of society.
- Children want and need to belong to the family unit. When positive means of belonging are denied or discouraged, a

child will misbehave as a means of establishing a place of importance within the family.

- Children learn early that they will get attention when they misbehave. They also discover that they will very likely get what they want, in spite of mom and dad's wishes, because they create such a disturbance their parents will give in to their demands.

- Low expectations by parents breed discouragement in children, which leads to more misbehavior.

- Many parental responses to children's misbehavior actually escalate the problems and power struggles, creating cycles of chaos and disturbance that become accepted patterns of behavior within the family.

- Empty threats, promises, emotional outbursts, and physical punishments such as spanking do not work to curb destructive patterns of family conflict.

- It is not necessary to reward, praise, or bribe children when they do the right thing. In fact, this can be just as disrespectful as yelling at them.

- Parents must honestly assess their own parenting styles to determine whether or not they fall into the "boss" or "permissive pal" category. Positive change for the whole family begins when parents accept that they must change their responses to their children's misbehaviors in order to change the family dynamics in positive ways.

- Establishing and following through with logical consequences for your children's misbehavior is essential to promoting positive change. Parents must be kind and firm when letting their children experience the consequences of misbehavior.

- Contribution is a vital element in teaching children positive ways to belong to the family and to society. Allowing your children to do chores, help make decisions, and take responsibility for obligations will give them a positive sense of importance and belonging.

# 2.

# Eating: Mealtimes at Home and Abroad

*"A child only behaves badly because he doubts his ability to get anywhere if he would behave himself."*

—RUDOLF DREIKURS

There seems to be a fairly new parenting phenomenon in many homes. Children dictate the how, when, what, and where of mealtimes. Adults routinely take turns acting as short-order cooks, fixing two and sometimes three different meals at a time so that their finicky children will find something to their liking on their plates.

Children are not expected to sit down at the table and eat the meal that is placed before them at specific hours of the day. Instead, they have been taught that if they do not want to eat what mom puts on the table, they need only sulk or complain and, voila!, something else will appear.

What is going on here? Why would a harried young mother put herself through the additional work of preparing special meals for her children as if she had all the time in the world at her disposal? And, taking this reasoning a step further, why, even if she did have ample time, would she consider it a good idea to cater to her children's unreasonable demands?

To answer that question, we must look at many different variables. First, mom, like many parents, has made a decision about how her children will be raised. Unfortunately, she has made that decision from a position of weakness, not of strength. Perhaps in her own past, she was made to eat whatever was put on the table and plenty of it. Now, whether consciously or unconsciously, she has determined that her children will never have to sit at a table choking down food they do not like because she is bigger and stronger than they are and can make them eat.

Acting not as a parent charged with providing nourishment for growing children but as a child rebelling against her own parents and their mealtime methodologies, this mom has trained her children to act like little tyrants at the table (if they are even sitting at the table!).

Parents must examine for themselves how they were raised and the decisions they have made about parenting based on their own experiences as children. They must investigate their behavior as children and the responses they witnessed from their own parents. All these factors provide clues that will help parents understand why they respond the way they do. This is a very important step in effecting change.

If we do not know why we do things, we cannot have much hope of altering them for the better. In order to change first ourselves and then influence change in our children's behavior, we need some insights into how and why we do certain things in certain ways.

As you engage in this process, you will have many of those "light bulb" moments where you begin to realize just what kinds of influences have formed and shaped your responses to your children. And you will also get a sense of whether or not these influences accurately reflect how you feel about things or the way that others think you should feel. This is a fundamental exercise for those of you who really want a deeper understanding of yourselves and your behaviors.

Consider, for example, that when parents do not act wisely with their own children, it is often because they are reacting based on something that was done to them and that has no bearing on what is the best training for their own children. They may still be rebelling, saying, "My parents did thus and such, and I will never do that to my children," instead of asking, "What things do my children need to learn from me in order to grow up to be healthy, happy, compassionate, and productive citizens?"

You do not need a list of the shortcomings of these old approaches for dealing with children, but it is essential to think for a moment about the conflict within your own family at specific times of the day, which are often centered around mealtimes. When properly used, these particular times of day need not split a family apart.

Instead, they can provide a sound foundation for growth and development by giving parents opportunities for educating and training children in such vital areas as communication, manners, sharing, contribution, and cooperation within the family.

Yes, you are tired. Yes, your children are overextended. Yes, cooking a good meal takes time and energy. You may even think it is easier to give them what they want when they want it because you have become accustomed to their whining, complaining, and refusals to eat what you put in front of them. If they are parked in front of the television with snack foods for meals because you cannot get them to join you for a real meal, you are losing all of these wonderful opportunities to:

- talk, visit, and relax with them during nonstressful times
- learn what they are thinking, doing, feeling
- work with them to learn to prepare meals
- teach them skills they will need as adults
- teach them about nutrition and how to feed themselves properly
- enlist their aid in tidying up after meals
- give them positive ways to contribute and help you
- enjoy their company and share things with them
- spend some cooperative time together that instills a sense of belonging

What parents also do not realize is that they are helping set up the dynamics for major power struggles in all areas when they cave in over meals and related activities. We must eat to live. No one will argue this point. However, the fact that you must feed your children allows them to use mealtimes as a chance to fight you for power and negative attention within the family.

That is why it is so important to look on mealtimes as a means of opening the door to positive modes of belonging. Since you, the parent, are the family leader, you can orchestrate the changes that will make mealtimes opportunities for cooperation rather than arenas of conflict.

It is really a very simple equation, and once you understand it, you can begin changing things. Responsible parenting requires that you provide nutritious food at specific times of each day. The only thing children have to do in order to make mealtimes the most upsetting times of the day is to refuse to eat. Since mealtimes occur more frequently throughout the day than other activities, eating becomes the most common area of conflict between parents and their children.

Children learn very early that their refusal to eat prompts certain responses from their parents. Good parents cannot let their children go without food, right? If children use their power and turn their noses up at the roasted chicken and green vegetables, they may be able to get their parents (after they have ranted and raved first) to offer them their favorite things like hot dogs and potato chips. Keep in mind the issue is not the chicken per se, the issue is the use of power to get a negative reaction from the parents.

Children are very smart when it comes to parental concerns over whether or not they eat. They know that when push comes to shove most parents will agree that it is better for children who are refusing the prepared meal to at least eat something, be it pizza, snack food, or, occasionally, even dessert.

It is very rare these days to find children thinking they had better eat what mom and dad have put on the table at specified mealtimes because otherwise they will have to go hungry until the next meal is served. But suppose that were the case? Let's look at how a typical scenario between parent and child might go:

*Jacob, nine years old, and his brother, seven-year-old Justin, are playing video games in Jacob's room. Mom and dad have prepared dinner, and now dad comes to Jacob's room and tells the boys to wash up and come to the table. They ignore him, engrossed in their games.*

*Dad tells them again, and they finally acknowledge his presence, telling him they are not hungry right now, and they want to finish playing their game. Dad tells them they can finish their game after dinner instead of helping to clean up if they will just come eat now. No response.*

*Now dad is angry. His own children will not do what he tells them to do. He begins shouting that unless they get to the table immediately, they will not be allowed to play video games for a week. Then he tells them they will go to bed hungry if they do not come eat right now.*

*Dad stomps off to dinner, but the two boys continue with their game. They know better than to believe either threat. They often refuse meals, knowing that their parents are very concerned that they eat.*

*They know mom will fix them something later when they complain of being hungry. They have no compunction about finishing the game they are enjoying instead of joining their parents at the dinner table.*

*They haven't learned about courtesy, cooperation, and contribution, nor will they as long as they continue to get away with this poor behavior.*

*Exasperated after waiting for the boys to do as they have been told, dad comes back and yells louder. Finally the kids come to the table where they poke and prod at their food, acting sullen and complaining that they hate the food that has been prepared for them.*

*It makes them sick. They cannot eat it. Their behavior spoils the meal for everyone. To top it off, they don't eat anything. When they finally leave the table, their plates are still full.*

*Later, after they have played their games and watched some television, they whine to mom that they are hungry and that they will not be able to sleep unless they get something to eat. They request giant soft pretzels with cheese melted on top, and then they plan to wheedle until they are also given some ice cream.*

*Though she is tired and has already put all the food away, mom goes back to the kitchen and prepares the snack they have requested. She has learned to have these items on hand since this scene is reenacted on a frequent basis.*

*Mom knows this kind of snacking is not really nutritionally sound, but at least they are eating something. That is what is most important, right?*

Why does this scene (and others like it) continue to get played out over and over? What could these parents do differently? What should they do differently? How many mealtimes will it take before they see that they are going through a rotating pattern of power struggles in which their children learn to be discourteous, disrespectful, and uncooperative?

In this instance, dad demonstrated anger and threats, common parental responses to children's misbehaviors. Parents embroiled in food fights with their children often contribute to the power struggle with these kinds of initial responses. But by getting angry, dad has reinforced their misbehavior because they were able to "get him going." Their bid for power has been successful.

If they persist in their misbehavior, they know they will most likely wear dad down and get what they want. This is the fundamental purpose of a power struggle. The child wins by persevering in the misbehavior until dad has had enough and gives in just to get the conflict over with.

Mother, on the other hand, demonstrates her doormat status by preparing the snack food. What is worse, the fact that she even has the snack food available, has gone out of her way to bring it into the house, indicates that she is anticipating the worst behavior (low expectations!) from her children.

This mom is actually encouraging the very behavior she does not want. In a sense, mom is also resorting to bribery, using snacks as substitutes for the meal she has prepared. This is tantamount to saying, "I will give you whatever you want if you will just eat something." If that is not bribery, what is?

What must the children think when every night mom is able to go into the kitchen and retrieve their favorite snacks? Do you think they get the message that she is prepared to dole out the rewards for their misbehavior as a matter of course? Yes, they do. Never forget that your actions send messages just as strong, sometimes stronger, than your words.

Another typical parental technique that is often used to get children to eat is guilt. For example, how many of us still cringe when someone jokes about the universal parental guilt trip that begins, "Think of the children starving in——— (fill in the blank with whichever country, city, or state your parents used!).

How many of us remember the old, "Clean your plate and you will get something good for dessert." Parents often make the mistake of trying to entice children to eat one item, such as a particular vegetable or kind of meat, by promising them a treat.

Another tactic parents use is micromanaging, which is the

practice of nagging, bragging, or begging every step along the way as children slowly consume a mouthful here and a mouthful there. How powerful is the child who can get mom to do this! And all he had to do to get it started was to show a lack of interest in eating. Here is what micromanaging looks like:

*Three-year-old Steven is dawdling over his supper. He is distracted by the television set in the background and toys lying near his feet. He sits and squirms, moving his food around for a few seconds, and then he gets up and roams around the room.*

*His mom spends the entire mealtime coaxing him to eat. She reads the paper distractedly while she keeps up a running monologue.*

*Mom says things like, "Just have one bit of chicken. See how good that is? How about one bean? Eat one bean, and then eat a bite of chicken. Did you drink any milk? Come back over here and have a piece of bread. Drink some milk now. Eat your bread with your milk." On and on she goes, prodding him down to the last nanopiece.*

How would you like to try and eat a meal with this going on? As adults, we tend to get insulted by this type of controlling, interfering behavior. Have you ever said, "I can cut up my own meat," as a way of letting someone know that they are micromanaging you? How much better would it be to disengage and let the child eat or not?

These clichés of parental control might seem humorous until we consider that, while the words may have changed, the parenting behaviors have remained the same. Some of these tactics to get children to eat may work on a short-term basis, but parents must not let brief bouts of success deceive them into thinking they are making headway with their children. To understand why all these tactics fail in the long run while sometimes achieving the results you want in the short run, let's revisit the scenario with Jacob and Justin.

What might mom and dad do differently if they finally decide to put an end to their children's tyranny and change the dynamics of their family's way of relating during mealtimes?

Let's assume that mom and dad have read this book, and now they have committed themselves to changing their relationships within the family. They will begin at mealtimes, working with their children to educate them as to the logical consequences that will follow when the children choose to misbehave. Mom and dad know that the first step in educating their children is to reeducate themselves. They must change their responses to their children's behavior in order to promote the changes they wish to see in their children.

The guiding principles mentioned in the introduction to this book begin here. As a parent, you must first recognize and admit that anger, emotional outbursts, conflict, and superficial threats do not work. If anything, you simply diminish yourself as a parent when you engage in these tactics.

Your children become stronger because they recognize they have gotten to you and made you lose your cool. On top of that, they have often actually manipulated you into giving them what they want.

Once you admit your current methods do not work, you open the door for new ideas, new approaches, and new behaviors. Change is very liberating once you accept it as a positive thing. Let go of the old and embrace the new. It will work for you. Now, consider this version of the Justin-Jacob scenario:

*Nine-year-old Jacob and seven-year-old Justin are playing a video game in Jacob's room. Dad comes to the door and asks them to please turn off the games and come to the kitchen to help prepare and serve dinner. The boys ignore him, expecting that, like every other night, he'll just yell at them and finally go away.*

*Tonight, dad says nothing when the boys ignore him. He simply walks into the room and, in a respectful way (no yelling, no threats, no emotion at all), he removes the video game from the room.*

*Now mom and dad are in the kitchen making dinner. The boys have not joined them but are sulking in Jacob's room. When the meal is on the table, mom and dad go about their business, eating the meal, discussing their day, and having a pleasant time together.*

*After eating, the parents tidy up, put the food away, and continue on with their evening's activities, ignoring the boys completely.*

*When Jacob and Justin come out and ask for pretzels and ice cream, mom and dad simply state once that dinner has been served and put away, and that the next meal is breakfast in the morning.*

*Once mom and dad deliver this message, they walk away and let the boys experience the consequences of their behavior. They did not help out in the kitchen as they were asked, nor did they come to the table and eat what had been prepared.*

*It is both logical and reasonable for the parents to ex-*
*pect the boys to have done both these things. When the*
*boys choose not to behave, the logical consequence is that*
*they have missed the meal and must now wait for the next*
*one.*

Horrors! The children must go to bed hungry? You must be the worst parents in the world! How can you not feed your hungry children? What will their grandparents say? What if they tell their teachers at school?

Put these images out of your head. You are not using starvation tactics to punish your children when you enact a consequence that includes a child's choice to miss a meal. What you are doing is taking an opportunity to teach them something important by simply allowing them to experience the consequences of their actions. Your job is to cook the meal. It is their choice whether to eat it.

You do them a great disservice when you do not prepare them to be independent and socially aware adults. You are not teaching them what to expect when they carry this same childish behavior forward into adulthood. What happens to a thirty-year-old who chooses not to eat a meal someone has prepared for him?

Will someone appear magically out of the woodwork to prepare something else or call the pizza delivery man so he can enjoy his favorite snack while others eat what has been served? Childhood is the time when we learn what promotes good relationships. If you do not provide these lessons for your children, who will?

Here's what will happen if you allow your children to face the consequences of not eating their dinners. They will go to bed hungry. When they get up the next morning, breakfast will look like a feast. They will eat heartily and appreciate every bite. In addition, they will possess some very practical knowledge about what happens when they make choices about eating. You may even see a vast improvement when they return home that day and eat dinner. The prepared meal may look much better this time around, and not because they have been punished, but because they have learned that their choices not to eat will be respected.

They now know that they will not be begged or threatened about eating. If they refuse to eat what is on the table at breakfast time, they will be hungry until the next meal is served. It will not seem like such a good idea the second time around because they now realize that mom and dad will not break out the snacks later on. Finally, they will have learned the most valuable lesson of all, that all choices have consequences.

This puts the ball back in their court, so to speak. It is their choice whether or not they go hungry, not yours. You are simply providing good, nutritious meals at certain times of the day. That is the extent of your responsibility as a parent. After that, it is up to them to take care of themselves by eating. When you put it in these simple terms, it is not difficult to understand, is it?

And yet many parents continue to fall back on old behaviors, thinking they are being good parents if they accomplish the task of making their children eat something. Contrast this "good" parent with the parent who instead chooses to take the time and go through the inconvenience of teaching the children a different kind of lesson. This parent knows that no good can come of placating or punishing, but a great deal of good can come from refusing to respond with punishment or bribes when children try to manipulate them.

Do you see how respectful this attitude is? If you are a parent who employs logical consequences, you are treating the children as individuals separate from you who have made a choice that you now let them live with. You are stepping back and letting them experience something on their own. That is an important stone in the foundation of education.

Once children have absorbed this lesson, why is it important to get them involved in the food preparation duties for the family? First of all, a central part of the Adlerian approach is to recognize the importance of each family member feeling as if he or she is making a substantial and important contribution to the family.

Everyone needs to feel useful. By letting children take part in the meal preparation, you are providing a way for them to express their usefulness as opposed to expressing their power over you.

There are so many things children can do, even very young children. They can help plan menus, set the table, carry food to the table, tear up lettuce for salad, or fill glasses with water. Older children can actually do some of the cooking. Children of almost any age can spoon out ice cream for dessert or carry something to the table.

And do not forget that when the meal is over, there are a great many chores that need to be done to set the kitchen to rights and tidy up. There may also be lunches to pack for the next day. Look on these tasks as opportunities for you to enlist your children in positive contributions that will help everyone. They can begin to feel important because of all the helpful things they do as opposed to feeling important because they "get your goat" by being disruptive and uncooperative.

And for those of you who have family pets, why not let these wonderful, loving creatures serve as props when you are teaching your children responsible mealtime behavior? Let your children take on the responsibility of preparing your pet's food, feeding the animal, and then cleaning up after the pet has eaten. This gives your child the opportunity to draw some parallels between the importance of Fido's eating behavior and his own.

Something as simple as letting him be responsible for your pet's feeding times also gives your child a positive, constructive mode of contribution within the family. The child is caring for the pet by providing nutrition, just as you are caring for your children by providing good meals for them. It does not take much for a child to make this connection and begin to see what this whole mealtime thing is all about.

It is impossible to stress enough the importance of giving children chores and responsibilities to complete for the family unit, for this is their means of belonging to the family and being important to the smooth functioning of the household. The feelings of self-worth a child will experience when he or she provides care for the family, four-legged members included, are part of the positive consequences of behaving well.

What tasks can your children assume in order to contribute to the whole process of preparing and eating meals? Think of these "golden opportunities" as gifts you can give your children and then allow even the youngest ones to help.

When children know their efforts are valued and appreciated, they will rise to the occasion no matter the task, and they will do as they are asked without sulking, complaining, or challenging. That is what having a place in the family is all about.

They will also learn to do the right thing even if no one notices. Their motivation becomes internal as opposed to external, where the focus is on being rewarded or punished. They do what needs to be done and feel good about it even if it does not attract the attention of their parents. Just take a moment and list the things your children could do to help you put meals on the table. Make a plan for your next meal together.

*Our next meal together will be* _____

*The menu we have planned includes*

_____

_____

_____

_____

_____

*My children (or my child) can help me by*

_____

_____

_____

_____

*Once the meal is over, my children (or my child) can help with clean up by*

_____

_____

_____

_____

Once you try this new approach, you will see results very quickly. Your own frustration levels will diminish because you are no longer yelling or threatening to no effect. You will be able to see their misbehavior as attempts to find significance as opposed to a personal affront, and this helps you control your feelings.

You can be calm and respectful with your children and detach yourself from the power struggles. That in and of itself brings about amazing changes in how you feel and how your children perceive you.

Over time you will see amazing changes in your children, as well. You must begin this new approach to parenting with courage and commitment. Recognize that investing time in your children now is preferable to the years of conflict and unhappiness that will result if you continue to relate to each other in the patterns you may have already established. You will have some wonderful years ahead of you if you put the time and effort into these changes now.

The logical place to begin these changes is at home, but you will find that often your children choose very public places in which to act out and engage in power struggles with you.

Let's talk about how to use some of the techniques and attitudes outlined so far when you take your children out to a restaurant and are confronted with the same old misbehaviors you are experiencing with eating at home.

## Eating Out: "These Children Aren't Mine, They're Just Sitting at the Table with Me."

That is probably what you'd like to say when you are sitting in a public place trying to have a meal and your children are misbehaving. It is very difficult to handle your children's finicky eating habits, pickiness, whining, complaining, balking at food choices that would be good for them, and doing what adults used to call "sassing" back at you as you try to get them to select something off the menu and then actually eat it.

Children may need smaller servings than adults, but other than that, menus should ideally dispense with special foods that are designed to appease finicky children by providing them with yet another opportunity to eat junk food. With that said, let's take a look at a scenario that is common in family restaurants today.

*Mom and dad have taken Nicole, age seven, Jenna, age nine, and Micah, age five, to the mall to shop for school clothes on a Saturday morning. They have stopped for lunch on the way home. Everyone is tired and hungry. The parents make their selections quickly, and then talk with the children about what they would like to eat.*

*Micah wants a hot dog, but there is no such offering on the menu. He insists that is the only thing he wants. He whines and complains even though it is pointed out to him over and over that this restaurant does not serve hot dogs. He sulks and refuses to make another choice.*

*Jenna wants a hot-fudge sundae and refuses to look at the other options on the menu. She insists she does not want any lunch, just dessert.*

*Nicole spills her water, says she wants a hamburger, retracts that and asks for spaghetti, then changes her mind several more times, refusing to settle on anything.*

*The waitress comes to take the order and is met with frazzled parents who are still trying to coax their little darlings into choosing something to eat.*

*By now all three children have decided they do not want lunch at all. They all want milk shakes and ice cream. They are begging and whining and causing a scene in order to get what they want. They know they can wear mom and dad down.*

*Dad finally loses patience and tells the waitress to bring them what they want. He is embarrassed by their behavior and just wants it to stop. If ice cream will do the trick, that is okay by him.*

*When the waitress leaves with the order, mom and dad tell the children they had better quiet down and eat their ice cream when it comes or they will return to the mall and take all their school clothes back to the stores.*

*The children quiet down, but when the food comes, they play with it rather than eating it, letting it melt in the dishes and drip on the front of their clothes. At least they are eating something, mom and dad rationalize. After all, ice cream is made from milk and milk is good for kids, right?*

*When this uncomfortable and unpleasant meal is finally over, the children have made a mess at the table, worn their parents out with their complaining, and, to top it off, they haven't eaten one nutritious thing. In addition, they have disrupted the meals of those sitting around them who have had to witness the arguing, sulking, and threatening.*

*When they get home, they complain about still being hungry and ask for soda and chips, which their parents let them have just to shut them up and gain a few moments' peace after their busy and tiring morning of shopping.*

It is embarrassing and annoying to be provoked to this kind of response by your own children in a restaurant, but these parents do not want to resort to the behavior they use at home when the children misbehave. They do not want to scream, fight, or spank in public. What would people think?

Children know parents do not want to engage in these behaviors in public, and knowing this gives them the upper hand for an expression of power. They know they can get what they want, ice cream, for example, so they go for it.

What is it about being out in public with misbehaving children that punches parental buttons? Perhaps it is the look of sympathy from the parents a table or two over from yours. Maybe it is the arched eyebrow and knowing look aimed at you by the well-groomed older lady who seems to be saying, "My children never behaved that way in public. You are really not in control of those little monsters." Maybe it is the feeling that you are being judged and labeled "bad parents" by onlookers who seem disgusted with your failure to produce well-behaved, happy little "Norman Rockwell" children who do everything beautifully and are a pleasure to observe.

Whatever it is, parents all seem to be much more comfortable when children are misbehaving at home and there are no witnesses around to see the parental flaws and failures that seem to be so magnified when they occur in public. We have already talked about changing your responses to your children's misbehavior at home. Guess what? The same principles apply when you are out in public.

If these parents read this book and embark on a strategy to change their family's dynamics at mealtimes, they will act very differently. When their children use the advantage of being out in public at a restaurant to try and engage in a power struggle with them, the parents will not fall for it.

Let's pick this family up at the point where the children have begun to complain about the menu. Here's what might happen if mom and dad rethink and redo their responses to their children's misbehaviors:

*Micah wants a hot dog, but there is no such offering on the menu. He insists that is the only thing he wants. He whines and complains even though it is pointed out to him over and over that this restaurant does not serve hot dogs. He sulks and refuses to make another choice.*

*Jenna wants a hot-fudge sundae and refuses to look at the other options on the menu. She insists she does not want any lunch, just dessert.*

*Nicole spills her water, says she wants a hamburger, retracts that and asks for spaghetti, then changes her mind several more times, refusing to settle on anything.*

*Dad turns to the misbehaving children and quietly announces, "We're leaving. We can tell by your behavior that you have decided for us to go. We will try again next time."*

*With that, mom and dad pick up and leave the restaurant and take the family home. They ignore the children's pleas to stay and do better. They do not explain, argue, or threaten. They simply leave, thereby stopping the power struggle before it can begin in earnest.*

*Once at home, mom and dad go about their normal routine. There will be no fighting, no anger, no threats, no complaining, no lecturing about what happened at the restaurant, and no lunch to replace the one they chose not to eat. Mom and dad will walk away from any and all discussions about the children's hunger.*

*They will enlist the children's help with dinner preparations and will put a good meal on the table. Their ex-*

*pectation is that their hungry children will contribute to the meal and will also eat it without complaint.*

*If this does not happen, the parents will not use anger, threats, pleading, or manipulation to get the children to eat. They will simply eat the meal themselves, put the food away, and continue with their day.*

*The children must wait for the next meal to be served in order to assuage their hunger. No anger, no lectures, no guilt-producing tactics. There is just action on the part of the parents, and that is all.*

Very powerful children will leave the restaurant and, once at home, go straight to the kitchen to try to prepare something to eat to make up for the meal they have missed. To make sure this doesn't happen once you have embarked on the new course, you should empty your kitchen of all the kid foods, snacks, and quick meals that your children have come to expect will be there. This is inconvenient, but you must keep in mind the long-term lesson you are teaching your children. For parents and children to make changes in behavior, it sometimes means making a commitment to the training process regardless of how inconvenient it is at first. You do need to plan ahead so that you are prepared once you begin the process.

If your kitchen is devoid of food the children like to eat and can fix quickly for themselves, you are ready for what might follow once you leave the restaurant. You continue to expect the best from your children, but you are prepared for the worst in case they push their power. Once again, you say nothing once you have enacted consequences.

Meals in restaurants give misbehaving children so many opportunities to challenge their parents and try to gain control of the situation. In addition to refusing to make a selection from the menu, children may be rude to their parents, to other family members, or to the restaurant staff.

They may make special demands for expensive or inappropriate menu items even though their parents have asked that they stick to specific kinds of food on the menu. They will most assuredly disturb the peace of those unfortunate diners seated around them.

But do not despair. Even very small children can learn to behave while dining in public. Children as young as two or three years old can learn to participate and enjoy these outings with the family and should be included in them. It is up to you to invest the time and follow through with the consequences in order in order to teach children how to behave in public. You can do it.

Parents need to remember a couple of things as they begin to implement these new behaviors. First of all, parents must remember that children are insightful about their misbehavior. Time after time, when children are asked why they misbehave, they invariably smile and explain that they know that is how they will get their way. They also admit that they know they can wear their parents down.

The second thing parents must remember is that it is of the utmost importance to have faith that your children will rise to the occasion. Even the worst-behaved children need to feel that you believe they can change and behave better. It is your job as a parent to make sure that these positive avenues are always available to your children.

When you do show faith, you let them know that it is their behavior you do not like and want them to change, not them. Even misbehaving children need to know their parents see their good qualities. This is an important part of feeling a sense of belonging and being accepted by your family.

Discouraging children is one of the most destructive things parents do. The implication is that because they are acting out in a specific instance they are beyond hope and cannot learn to behave better. How many times have you said, "I will never take you to ———— again"? This can be a devastating message to children and goes to the core of their feelings about themselves the first time that they hear you say it. After that, it becomes part of a habitual pattern of communication and has no effect on them. It simply becomes part of the game.

On the other hand, your expectation that your children can and will do better even though they are not acting correctly during this particular instance exhibits tremendous faith in them as people. Your faith will be rewarded if you let your children know in calm and rational terms that you have high expectations for them the next time even though they may not be acting as you wish at this particular moment. You are teaching your children what good behavior is and that you expect they will change their behavior willingly in order to contribute to the family.

Remember that there are positive consequences for your children to experience, as well as negative ones. That is why it is important to let your children know that even though you are leaving the restaurant this time, you believe they will do better next time. Then give them that opportunity, but be prepared to deal with whatever the child's behavior may be.

The consequences of good behavior are that the child will be part of the family meal and will enjoy a nice time in the restaurant. They begin to get a taste of belonging positively. This is

encouraging, especially for those children who have been labeled "bad" or a "problem."

And remember not to confuse this process with the "second
chance" option, which is a parental mistake brought about by a
contrite child. Once misbehavior occurs, there is no second
chance at that time. However, there is the expectation that the
next time (tomorrow, next week, next month) the child has the
opportunity to behave in the right way, he or she will do so.

Part of the idea of contribution is that through thinking of
others, children learn to make positive choices that benefit the
family. A child who is helping the family by behaving well and
is proud of the way his or her behavior benefits others, is a child
who will not choose to misbehave.

Here are the most effective ways to deal with misbehavior in
restaurants:

- The minute a child misbehaves in the restaurant, the family
  leaves. In a calm and respectful tone, the parents say, "We
  see by your behavior you have decided for us to leave. We
  will try again next week." And then they leave. No anger, no
  threats, no cajoling, no lectures. The parents simply take action, and the child experiences the consequences of misbehavior.
- Plan ahead and take two cars to the restaurant. One parent
  may employ the consequences mentioned above and leave
  with the misbehaving child while the rest of the family stays
  and enjoys dinner.
- In the car on the way home, say nothing about what has just
  happened in the restaurant. The parent driving home can
  remain silent but with a friendly demeanor. Let the child

figure it out. Do not fuss, criticize, or reiterate what will happen when the child misbehaves. There is no need for a further consequence. The child knows.

- Let your children know they will have another opportunity to go out to eat with the family and that you are sure they will behave the next time. Children must know that they haven't "blown it" by misbehaving once or twice. They must know they will have a chance to redeem themselves and behave properly next week.
- There is no second chance for this time, though.

We have already talked about how a child can contribute when the meals are being prepared and served at home, but what are some ways a child may contribute to the family's meal in a restaurant?

For one thing, a child might help a younger sibling decipher the menu and choose food items that are in line with mom and dad's budget and nutritional requirements.

You might like to let the child place the order with the waiter once family members have made their decisions about what they would like to eat. You might want to give the money to the child at the end of the meal and let him go up to the cashier and pay the bill and return the change to you.

The basic rules for encouraging good behavior are simple:

- Take action immediately when a child misbehaves the first time so that he or she experiences the consequences.
- Create positive ways for your children to contribute to the family no matter what activities you are involved in.
- Expect that your children will want to belong to the family

in positive and well-behaved ways, and keep giving them opportunities to do so.

Perhaps the most important part of this kind of parenting is your ability to control your responses to your children's behaviors to avoid any kind of power struggle, arguing, shouting, yelling, punishing, threatening, cajoling, or giving in. Be a calm, kind, firm, and respectful parent.

When you do that, you are modeling for your children the behaviors you expect that they will exhibit, both in public and in the privacy of your own home. You are also modeling self-control, which is what you really want your children to exhibit most of all.

Parents are the first and greatest role models a child encounters. And if you are in doubt of that, look carefully at your children's misbehaviors and see how closely they mimic your own responses to things. All the yelling, threatening, cajoling, and manipulating may sound very familiar.

You were operating from a different set of ideas about parenting when you modeled these behaviors in the past. Now you can do something new, and the behavior you model will accomplish positive things for your children.

To get this process started, remember that you will not be able to make the changes necessary to truly help your family function more smoothly and lovingly unless you honestly assess your own behaviors and responses. This will help you determine what you must do to make changes for yourself that you can then model and teach your children.

It is not easy to be this honest with yourself. But it is essential. Once you commit yourself to changing your relationship with your children, you will find the strength to do what you need to do.

It is important to reiterate that change must begin with you. Your self-control, your tone of voice, and your level of respect will all be communicated to your children as you begin to make changes in the way your family interacts. You are going to be amazed at how much better you feel, how much more control you have over your emotions, and how much you can lower your stress levels just by taking hold of your responses to your children's misbehaviors.

The great thing about focusing in on specific problem areas such as the three this book targets is that they give us a place to begin making changes that we can adapt to all parts of our lives. If the journey of a thousand miles begins with a single step, then the journey to helping your children achieve happy, productive lives can begin with teaching them how to behave respectfully at the table.

## This Chapter in a Nutshell

- Parents are the earliest and most influential role models for children.
- Everyone must eat, and children sense early on that not eating is a weapon that can be used against concerned parents who worry about their children's health.
- Children can learn to eat the meals that are prepared for them at specific times of day. They do not need special food or enticing treats to cajole them into eating good, healthy food.

- Your children will not starve if they miss a meal or two. They learn from the consequences of their choosing not to eat.
- Children can contribute to family mealtimes by helping plan, set up, and create food for family meals. They can make their own school lunches as well. They can also make substantial contributions to the family by helping with cleanup after each meal.
- Children can learn to behave well and make good, nutritional food choices no matter whether they are dining at home or eating at a restaurant. The same principles for training children to behave positively work effectively when employed at home or out in public.
- The keys to changing mealtime from a battleground to a pleasant arena for productive family interactions are to be found in parental reactions to a variety of children's misbehaviors at mealtime.

# 3.

---

# Sleeping: Ending Bedtime Battles

*"If you do something for a child that he can do for himself, you take away the child's responsibility towards life."*

—RUDOLF DREIKURS

Parents who are already exhausted from busy days of work and child-rearing responsibilities have become increasingly accustomed to the nerve-wracking routine that has developed around getting their children into bed. They have come to expect that these bedtime battles are one more torturous part of the day that must be gotten through before they can finally collapse into bed themselves.

Yes, you must have a routine for getting your children to bed on time each night. But do not make the mistake of thinking it must be an excruciating, wearying, hours-long process. This may be your pattern now, but it does not need to be the way you continue to do things. Once you admit that your current routine is not helping anyone, then you can begin to change it.

Your children desperately need their sleep. Their days, like yours, are chock-full of activities ranging from school to extracurricular activities to homework to chores. You know how exhausted you are after a long and busy day; your children are tired, too. That is why it is so important to establish a solid routine that gets your children to bed without a fight. They need their sleep, just as you do. Without that refreshing eight or so hours, will any of you be able to tackle all the tasks waiting for you tomorrow? Here's an example of what is happening in families all over America:

*A young father, who is devoted to his four-year-old son, arrives at work ten to fifteen minutes late every morning. He is, of course, apologetic to everyone about his tardiness, and, to date, hasn't attracted the notice of his supervisor, though how much longer he can continue arriving late, fatigued, and red-eyed is anyone's guess.*

*This dad always has a long story to tell, and it never varies. He begins his apologies by reminding everyone that Tommy just will not go to sleep at night. He's a "night owl" and he just refuses to go to bed.*

*He keeps his mother and father up until all hours with his chatter and activity. This young dad then explains that he, himself, was "just like that" as a child. He, too, refused to go to bed, was a "night owl," and ruled the roost each evening by keeping his parents up until all hours.*

Of course, the explanation for his lateness every day is a predictable one. Because they have all gone to bed quite late, nobody is able to get up and get going the next morning. This is the topic of the next chapter, but the important point to bear in mind here is that lack of sleep creates a whole new set of problems that is going to play out all day long for all members of this family.

This young man often talks about how his four-year-old is just like a "little old man" in his words and behaviors. He takes delight in relating some of the humorous things this precocious child says and does, relishing the irony of a small child who acts out adult characteristics.

Clearly, this young father and his wife are not acting respectfully and responsibly when it comes to bedtime for their child. What they are doing is indulging this little boy. At the same time, they are explaining away their lack of parenting skills by attributing adult characteristics to the child and categorizing the child's misbehavior as part of some genetic pattern that emerges in the bloodlines of dad's family.

"I was just like that as a child" is not an adequate excuse for a child's misbehavior. Your child may have your eye color or the same texture of hair, but acting out is not a genetic trait. Indeed, this kind of rationalizing merely points out a pattern of parental weakness that is being carried forward into another generation. Why would an intelligent man accept this kind of thinking and continue indulging and spoiling a child he clearly loves and wants to raise responsibly?

The plain truth is that even though continuing battles with misbehaving children are difficult and exhausting, most parents think that it is actually easier to endure these horrendous, upsetting cycles of conflict than it is to change them. Change is frightening to people, especially to parents who feel they will do or say the wrong things and scar their children for life. It is easier to say, "I was like that as a kid," than it is to confront the fact that maybe your parents modeled the wrong responses that you have now adopted as you cope with your own children.

Breaking cycles of behavior is not easy, especially when we see that behavior in terms of how our parents raised us. However, if you are worn out from this kind of conflict with your children, you are ready for change. It is okay to recognize that you may need to do things differently from the way your parents did them. It is essential to recognize this when your child's misbehavior is having an adverse impact on the whole family.

The young dad arrives at work late, tired, and apologetic every day. It is likely that he will soon receive a reprimand of some kind from his supervisor. Perhaps that will be a wake-up call to him that something must be done to get the child back on track. If these parents do not take steps to address this situation soon, their son will enter school without ever changing his bad habits. He will be one tired little boy every morning when his school day begins. And, if the pattern continues to hold, he'll probably be tardy every day, too, just like dad.

Are his parents doing him a favor by allowing him to control the sleep patterns of the family? Are they helping him to learn about responsibility, punctuality, or respect for others? Are they teaching him how to take care of himself properly by allowing adequate sleep time to replenish his energy and maintain his health? More important, are they teaching him how to be a respectful, responsible father when he, himself, has little ones?

Parents like these need to become aware of the troublesome patterns they are encouraging. Otherwise, they will be guilty of producing another generation of fatigued children with indulgent parents who have plenty of excuses and rationalizations to explain why they cannot get to work on time or contribute fully to their jobs and in their lives.

Added to that, a four-year-old "little old man" may be charming and amusing to his indulgent parents, but a teenager who exhibits these kinds of misbehaviors is nothing to chuckle about. It is vital to act as responsible parents who are loving yet firm in establishing consequences and following through with the kind of discipline that teaches children how to behave in the social world.

The process of teaching children about going to bed on time and staying in bed so that they get the sleep they need is a perfect exercise in teaching cooperation, contribution, and responsibility. It is also a golden opportunity for enacting consequences so that children learn what happens when they do not do the things they need to do to help the family unit function smoothly and efficiently.

Always remember that with each area of focus, such as bedtime, you are actually working on a much larger philosophical change that you will eventually incorporate into everything your family does together.

Your bedtime routine need not be relegated to the half hour before you expect your child to go to sleep. In fact, the more time you allot for this activity, the less harried it will become. The routine you wish to establish may actually begin early in the evening. Your first step toward getting your children ready for bed may be getting them involved in preparing school lunches for the next day.

Dinner is over, homework is done, and now the process of getting ready for tomorrow must begin. Young children who are off to day care in the mornings, can help prepare their lunches or snacks for the next day, even if all they do is help mom or dad put graham crackers in a Baggie. They are learning about the process of taking care of themselves by getting ready for tomorrow, all of which is part of the bedtime routine you are establishing.

Remember that every small act you encourage your child to perform is an experience that will begin to teach independence and responsibility. Children should know that if they do not get to bed on time, they will be disrupting the family's ability to have a calm, relaxing evening that helps prepare for the rigors of the day to come. No child should be allowed to think it is okay to disrupt a family's evening for selfish reasons.

Let's look at some scenarios and some solutions. Do a serious reality check here and pay close attention to those examples that seem most familiar to the routines your own family has established.

*Four-year-old Katie knows that bedtime is approaching, but she ignores her mother's repeated requests that she brush her teeth, wash her face, and don her nightgown.*

*Katie begins to whine that she wants to watch television and stay up like her older sister. Mother is exhausted after a full day's work and an evening of meal preparation, homework supervision, and kitchen cleanup.*

*She feels she is just too tired to argue with Katie, so she tells her she can stay up an extra half hour if she promises to go to bed right after the next television program is over.*

*Katie agrees, but, of course, when that half hour ends and another television program begins, she forgets her promise. She begins to dawdle, whine, and bargain for more time. Because mom didn't address the problem the first time around, it is now coming back to haunt her.*

*Katie won the first round and got to stay up the extra half hour. What is more, it was not all that hard for her to get her way. Why wouldn't she try it again?*

*Now mother is out of patience completely. She loses her temper, yells at Katie, and threatens to take away all television watching for the next week if the child does not get to bed right away.*

*Katie grudgingly leaves the family room and goes off to get ready for bed. She dawdles in the bathroom, playing with toothpaste and making a mess. She takes her own sweet time about changing into nightclothes and keeps repeatedly asking her mother for things like glasses of water, bedtime stories, and goodnight kisses.*

*Mother complies with all of Katie's demands. She gives her a glass of water, reads her a story, tucks her in, gives her several good-night kisses. After all, she is a good mom, right? What kind of parent refuses a child a good-night kiss?*

*However, every time mom thinks that is the end of it and leaves Katie in her room to fall asleep, Katie gets up and comes back out, asking for a snack or telling mom she is afraid of the dark.*

*By this time, Katie is crying, mom is frazzled, and the situation has nowhere to go but downhill. Mom finally blows her top, marches Katie to bed, and tells her she will not be allowed to play outside with her scooter if she does not stay in bed.*

*Katie responds with a full-blown crying tantrum, knowing mom's threats will never be carried out. Mom*

*comes back into the room and spends time calming Katie*
*down so that she can finally go to sleep.*

*Katie has gotten a lot of attention, and she has won*
*the power struggle with mom. On top of that she knows*
*mom will not follow through with her threat about the*
*scooter.*

*Mom is exhausted but feels she has achieved a small*
*victory in that Katie is at least finally asleep.*

Do not be satisfied with this kind of small victory in the continuing battles with your children. Recognize that these are major power struggles, and that, if you are responding to these misbehaviors the same way Katie's mother chooses to respond, you are *losing*.

Furthermore, you are teaching your children that their particular brand of selfishness, lack of appreciation for others, and emotional outbursts will work in the battle to get their way. Imagine how your children will look and sound as adolescents and adults if they continue on this path.

Many parents who are having difficult times with their teens are living this nightmare right now because they did not establish different ways of doing things when their children were younger. They can still succeed in changing things and creating better relationships with their teenage children, but it takes longer and it is more difficult to change patterns that have been in place for years and years. You have the advantage if you are making these changes when your children are much younger.

And remember that, just like the young father we discussed earlier, you are establishing parenting patterns that your children will carry forward into the next generation. "Oh, yes, I was just like that as a child" will become your children's theme as they parent their own offspring into the same cycle of misbe-havior and unhappiness your family is enduring right now.

Let's revisit Katie and her mother and talk about what could be done and what kinds of consequences might be established in this situation. First of all, it is clear that this is a battle played out regularly with Katie and her mother. It is so predictable that it has become a little like a staged play. It is a game. They both know their lines and what comes next in the series of events that constitutes the family drama, "Bedtime for Katie."

Regardless of the number of times they have played out this scenario, however, Katie's mother can still rewrite the script and make the changes needed to end this frustrating cycle of events. Mom needs to stand firm immediately. When Katie first asks to be allowed to stay up an extra half hour, mother must calmly but firmly say, "No." Mom does not need to explain her decision to hold Katie to her structured bedtime. Mother must simply deny the request and tell Katie to brush her teeth and get into bed. If Katie refuses to do what she knows she should do, mother can unplug or remove the television or game or what-ever is in the way of Katie getting ready for bed.

When Katie dawdles and ignores mother's request that she brush her teeth, mother should give Katie a limited choice. "Do you want to brush your teeth, or do you want me to brush them?" This choice is given in a calm, respectful way, not in a threatening, hostile, "If you do not do it, I will do it for you!" kind of tone.

If Katie does not make the choice and brush her own teeth, mom gets the toothbrush and follows through by brushing Katie's teeth for her without further comment. One way or an-other, tooth brushing is accomplished at the time it should be. This same approach can be applied to face washing and dressing in pajamas. The child may choose to do it, or she may choose for mom to do it. Either way, the tasks are completed at the right time.

After observing the nightly routine of one bedtime story, one drink of water, and one kiss good-night, mom is done. She now turns out the light and leaves Katie in her room to fall asleep. She need not interact further with Katie. Mom needs to move on to the other tasks of the evening.

These basic responses are serving two purposes. First, mom's new behavior is getting the tasks of preparing for bed done on time. Mom does not respond to whining, wheedling, or dawdling. When it comes to important health or safety items such as brushing teeth, it is appropriate for the parent to give the child limited choices of how they may accomplish the task. Mom gives Katie limited choices in a matter-of-fact tone. "You can choose to do these things, or you can choose for me to do them. Which is it?"

When the child does not get going with the tooth brushing, it is an indication that she has decided that her mother should do it. The point is that these things must be done. However, the parent need not bully or bribe the child into doing them.

Without the customary fighting, dawdling, or bargaining, you can see right away that the evening's process of readying children for bed has been shortened considerably. But notice something else. Mom's responses to the situation have made it possible for bedtime tasks to be accomplished without anger, threats, pleas, escalating temper tantrums, or fighting of any kind on her part.

Already, she feels better about the whole process. She is less fatigued mentally and physically, and she is acting in the way a parent should, firmly, respectfully, and wisely. Mom feels renewed self-confidence in the way she has handled things, and that is also a good reason for implementing these new ways of doing things.

The child might still be throwing a temper tantrum in the other room, but consider this new possibility. The tantrum is Katie's problem. Mom does not have to do anything about that. She has done everything a responsible parent is supposed to do. Her job is finished. The child may be making a disturbance in her room, but mom can ignore that.

Letting Katie throw a tantrum that does not generate a response from mom is a respectful way of demonstrating consequences. The tantrum does not help Katie get what she wants. Mom does not respond in the old ways that Katie has come to expect. Soon, the child will realize that these tantrums do nothing but make her feel bad, and she will simply stop throwing them because they are not achieving any desired results.

The cycle is broken, and everybody feels much better at day's end. These kinds of changes do not happen overnight, but you will begin to see and feel immediate results once you start responding differently, even if only within yourself. That is because you will not be putting yourself through the exhausting and emotionally draining power struggles you have been engaging in with your children.

The benefit of ending conflict is immediate for the mom and dad who simply detach from the battles with their children while holding firm and letting children experience the consequences of their choices.

The earlier point made about positive belonging applies here. Children want to feel important and productive within the family. When children are given the choice of doing a task such as brushing their own teeth or having it done by mom or dad, they will usually rise to the occasion and do it themselves. None of us likes to have someone else assume our responsibilities and do everything for us, least of all children who want to master more and more skills and increase their autonomy.

Children take immense pride in being able to do things for themselves, especially when they can show mom and dad how grown up they are. For their part, mom and dad do not need to heap praise upon the heads of children who do what is expected of them, but they can acknowledge the child's efforts. This is how parents nurture positive feelings of belonging. They acknowledge that the child has been helpful by doing the tasks required by saying something like, "You went to bed on time last night and that was a big help to me."

And since we're talking about how children like to emulate their parents, we can take a minute here to review a fundamental parental responsibility, which is to model the desired behavior so that your children can see it in action. This means that you, too, must order your evening bedtime activities, get enough sleep, and prepare for the coming day to avoid being harried and stressed.

Before you begin reorganizing your children's bedtime routine, do you need to do some work on your own? Think about how you spend the time at home after work. Do you procrastinate, watch too much television, snack instead of preparing meals, dawdle and put off going to bed until the last possible minute?

Remember, positive change within the family begins first with the parents. Recognize your role as a model of behavior. Do not be a "do as I say, not as I do" kind of parent. If you have not made some positive changes in yourself first, then it is difficult for your children to understand why you want them to change their behavior.

However, once you are in command of your own time and are doing some good modeling, realize that you can expect your children to stop misbehaving and do what you ask them to do when it is time for them to do it. Also remember that there need be no lengthy explaining, yelling, threatening, or conflict of any kind. Assume your children know what you expect them to do. Give your children limited choices and then do what you must do to achieve the necessary results.

## Homework Headaches

One sure-fire way to lower stress before bedtime and improve your quality of life is to get out of the homework business every evening. Parents often say that they are resentful at the amount of homework their children have. They feel it takes away from family time. Teachers who buck the system often agree with these parents and feel children are overburdened.

Many parents have assumed the responsibility for making sure the homework gets done correctly, and packed up for the next day. This usually means a battle royal with their children. Several things happen on the homework front each night.

First of all, many children resist doing their homework. They may even tell their parents they do not have any homework. Then they watch television or play games until just before bedtime when they "suddenly" recall that ream of paper in their backpacks.

Mom and dad have two choices. They can let the child stay up late and do the homework, which means they will be up with him since he needs help. Or they can say, "Oh, well. I guess you will not be able to do your homework because it is too late. It is time for you to go to sleep."

Usually parents go with the first choice. They help the child, who is staying up late, and will have trouble themselves getting up in the morning. Parents are so overinvested in their children's homework that they simply cannot stand back and let the consequences occur.

And, even when the child begins the homework at a reasonable hour and does not try to delay doing it, battles will erupt. Parents hear the child's frustration with assignments that are difficult or demanding, and they go in to check on his progress. Children often take their homework frustrations out on their parents, who are only trying to help. Sometimes the child tries to get the parent to actually do the work. And some parents will leap in to rescue their children by doing it.

Children will also verbally abuse whoever is trying to help them. Instead of walking away from this abuse as they should, many parents stay and take it because they are too involved in ensuring that their children do not get into trouble the next day at school. Once again, parents worry that they will be looked upon as bad parents because little Tommy is not ready for class.

In the "old days," it never occurred to parents to get involved in their children's homework issues except on very rare occasions. They thought it was the child's work and responsibility. What happened?

In the first place, children have more homework now and are often overwhelmed. There is so much emphasis on testing and evaluating school districts based on student performance that many children are feeling pressured from the time they enter first grade.

Parents have also contributed to the problem by wanting their children to be at the "top of the heap" in all ways. They are already planning their child's college future and the kid is only seven years old. And do not think the children do not feel this pressure, too. They do.

What to do? How do you handle the pressure that comes home in a backpack every night? Well, you do not. This is your child's responsibility. The homework is an issue between the child and the teacher.

What you can change is your response to the homework hassles. Try these approaches:

- Let your child know that it is his or her responsibility to get the homework home in the backpack, do it early in the evening, and get it back to school on time.
- Help your child with suggestions about how to organize the study area and the backpack.
- Set yourself up as a consultant only. You will help as requested, but you will not do the work or take responsibility for it getting done.
- The moment you are abused with back talk, whining, or eye rolling you are done "consulting" for that night.
- Nothing (tears, panic, remorse, bargaining) draws you back in to help.
- Change your philosophy. Work on yourself to change your values about the importance of the homework. In other words, do not end up doing the work yourself so that your child's grade will be higher. This is disrespectful to your child. The message to the kid is, "You need me to rescue you so that it will be done right."
- Give up fighting about homework altogether. If it does not

get done, your child will have consequences at school the next day. Let the child experience the consequences.

Do not let the homework issue become the major battle of the evening. It stresses you and your children out, and it diverts you from doing other tasks that are important. Also, the extra stress may be interrupting everyone's sleep. No wonder parents and children cannot get up in the morning.

Let's look at another scenario which encompasses a whole evening in the life of one family and determine what might be done differently by these parents:

*Mom has arrived home at 6:00 P.M., having picked up her seven-year-old son Brian from T-ball practice. Dad arrives about six-fifteen with eight-year-old Kari, who's been at a music lesson.*

*The children have dumped their school papers and backpacks on the kitchen table and run off to the family room to watch television. Mom and dad are in the kitchen preparing dinner.*

*Mom calls to the children and asks them to take their things to their rooms. They yell back that they will do so, but they do not come get the papers and packs.*

*Dinner is ready, and mom carries the children's things to their rooms. Then she calls them to come wash up and eat dinner. After some hesitation and grousing, they do so.*

*Dad tells the children they need to turn off the television set after dinner and do their homework. They complain that their favorite program is on tonight. Then they tell dad they do not have any homework due tomorrow. It can all wait until the weekend.*

*They do not eat much, and then go back to the television, leaving mom and dad to clean up the kitchen.*

*A short while later, mom tells the children it is time to get ready for bed. By now, she is tired and impatient. The children do not respond to her request because they are watching television, so she has dad go in and tell them again to get ready for bed.*

*Dad, too, is tired from a long day. In addition, he has some office projects he must work on at home tonight. He goes back to the den to do his work. The children stay put in front of the television.*

*Mom comes back in and tells the children once more to get ready for bed. They grumble and mumble, but get up and go to their rooms to change into their pajamas.*

*Mom checks back a few minutes later and finds they are playing games in Brian's room. They haven't brushed their teeth or washed their faces.*

*Mom demands that they cease playing and get their teeth brushed. It takes another forty-five minutes to actually get this task accomplished, with mom having to come back in every few minutes and prod them along.*

*When they are finally in bed, the getting up and down begins. Brian suddenly remembers that he does have a homework paper that must be turned in tomorrow. He gets up to rummage around in his backpack to find it.*

*Kari remembers that there is a field trip tomorrow to a local museum all morning. The children are supposed to pack lunches to eat in the museum's outdoor picnic area.*

*Mom rushes to fix Kari a lunch and help Brian finish his homework. Then she begins the process of getting them into bed all over again. When they balk, she loses her tem-*

*per and threatens that she will not let Kari go on the field trip if they do not get to bed right now.*

*Dad hears the yelling and wades into the fray, telling the children they are distracting him. If he does not get his work done, he says, he'll lose his job, and then they will all be homeless. The children giggle. They have heard this one before.*

*Dad becomes even more incensed and gives Brian a swat, sending him off to bed crying. Kari dives beneath the covers before he can turn in her direction, but she is crying, too, by now.*

*Mom and dad end up having an argument about whether or not parents should spank children. By the time they stop arguing and dad finishes his work, it is very late, they are exhausted.*

The wearing down of parents and children by this repeated cycle of selfishness, lack of contribution and cooperation, and escalating tempers is what fuels daylight-to-dark battles about sleeping, eating, and getting up. One problem spirals into the others until peace within the family seems impossible. How can there be calm, respectful communication when nothing but chaos surrounds these basic activities? The worst thing that happens is that adults and children become used to the pattern of conflict and soon begin to believe there is no other way to conduct family activity.

Parents who have endured these chaotic cycles for some time and have simply grown used to relating to their children and to each other this way have lost all perspective. When these patterns become the routine, the greatest problem for parents who now want to change things is where to begin. The task can seem overwhelming, but take heart. It does not matter where you start, only that you *do* start.

Let's take our long, involved scenario above and deconstruct it from beginning to end. Step by step, we will look at the dynamics of this family and how they are setting the stage for bedtime problems from the moment they enter their home at the end of the day.

> *Mom has arrived home at 6:00 P.M., having picked up her seven-year-old son Brian from T-ball practice. Dad arrives about six-fifteen with eight-year-old Kari, who's been at a music lesson.*

After long days at work and full days of school augmented by extracurricular activities that many parents feel children must have, it is no wonder evenings are so hectic. Children and parents are suffering from a strange twenty-first century malady that could be called being "wired and tired." After so much activity and stimulation, it is not a mystery, fatigued though they may be, that adults and children have trouble sleeping at night.

A first step you might take as a parent is to ask yourself how many after-school activities are really important to your children's well-being. Choose, with your child, one or two things he or she may take part in and eliminate some of the stress you, your spouse, and your children feel, which will make a difference in the kinds of evenings you can expect to have as a family.

> *The children have dumped their school papers and backpacks on the kitchen table and run off to the family room*

*to watch television. Mom and dad are in the kitchen preparing dinner.*

*Mom calls to the children and asks them to take their things to their rooms. They yell back that they will do so, but they do not come get the papers and packs.*

Children need not head directly for the television set on arriving home. If this is what is happening in your family right now, it may be one of the first things you want to change. You may decide that the television is off-limits for everyone, parents included, until after dinner.

Evenings can be a very productive family time for you and your children, but not when you all go to your separate corners and ignore one another. A basic opportunity for contribution can come at mealtimes, as we have discussed in the previous chapter on eating. The children can and should be in the kitchen helping get the meal on the table.

This is an ideal time to talk about school, homework that is due, problems and family issues that have arisen, and plans for the next day. It is a time for sharing and interacting. And, of course, it goes without saying that the first thing the children should do when they arrive home is put their school papers and backpacks in designated areas such as their rooms or the family room. This is where consequences come in. For example, if the children do not pick up their packs and books before you start preparing dinner, you can do several things.

Since your children have chosen not to take these items to their rooms, and you have to pick them up because they are in the way of your work, you remove them to a location such as the garage, the trunk of the car, or the top of the closet. The items are yours now since you had to move them. Be ready for the children to protest that they need their homework and that you are a horrible parent for hiding their belongings.

Remain calm. Do not explain or respond. They know what has happened. And they see the logic of your response, even though they will likely not admit it. However, they will learn not to leave their backpacks out. You have to be tough with yourself and follow through. You need to be willing to allow the children to feel the consequences and all the ramifications, which include going to school without a backpack the next day.

Another consequence is that you cannot cook in a cluttered kitchen. So you sit down and put your feet up. There is no dinner. When the kids want to know why you are reading a novel instead of preparing dinner, you say, "I can't work in a cluttered kitchen." And you continue to sit and read. Do not respond to their cries and protestations of being hungry or arguments about whose fault it is that you are not cooking.

The consequences your children will experience by organizing their things are pleasant ones. They will be able to find what they need when they need it. You will be teaching them to create order and routine in their lives. You, in turn, will not have to try to work around the clutter that results when they leave these items all over the kitchen.

Even very young children can be taught that part of their contribution to the smooth-running family evening is to take responsibility for their things and put them away as soon as they get home. Otherwise, they are creating disorder for everyone else.

Since we have already covered mealtimes and eating in an earlier chapter, you should be able to spot right away the problems at this point in the scenario. You have already considered what measures a respectful, responsible parent will take when children behave in this way at mealtimes. Let's pick this family up after dinner at the point that the children are supposed to be getting ready for bed.

> *A short while later, mom tells the children it is time to get ready for bed. By now, she is tired and impatient (because she hasn't successfully dealt with their finicky, rude behavior during the evening meal). The children do not respond to her request because they are watching television, so she has dad go in and tell them again to get ready for bed.*
>
> *Dad, too, is tired from a long day. In addition, he has some office projects he must work on at home tonight. He goes back to the den to do his work. The children stay put in front of the television.*

First of all, mom should not rely on dad to provide the "muscle" to get the children to do what she asks. If she does not have her own ability to enact consequences with the children, now is the time to establish it. Mom can simply enter the room and turn off the television set, leaving the children with two choices: sit in a quiet room or get ready for bed. She does not need to explain herself or listen to their complaints. Her actions speak louder than words, and her children know exactly what message she is sending.

Mom can then go about her business and expect that her children will get ready for bed. She needs to complete all these actions calmly, respectfully, and quietly. There should be no threats or declarations about how and why the set is going off. It is perfectly all right to say simply, "I'm turning off the television because it is time for you to get ready for bed." If the children turn the set back on, then the television is removed from the room without comment.

But why are the children choosing to go straight to the television set after dinner? There is cleanup to be done, and the children need to be part of this process. They need to help the family by doing their share. Let's continue on with this scenario.

*Mom comes back in and tells the children once more to get ready for bed. They grumble and mumble, but get up and go to their rooms to change into their pajamas.*

*Mom checks back a few minutes later and finds they are playing games in Brian's room. They haven't brushed their teeth or washed their faces.*

*Mom demands that they cease playing and get their teeth brushed. It takes another forty-five minutes to actually get this task accomplished, with mom having to come back in every few minutes and prod them along.*

It is time for the parent to give the children some simple choices. Using a respectful tone and a mild, nonhostile manner, mom can announce to the children that their options are to do the face-washing and tooth-brushing routines by themselves or choose to have these things done for them by the parent. Then quietly follow through by performing these actions if need be.

It is important to remember that now is not the time for any second chances. If the child is not putting the washcloth to his face, then that is an indication he has chosen for the parent to do it. If the child changes his mind once mom begins the face washing and begs to do it himself, the parent continues the task and says, "We will see how it goes tomorrow."

These words show faith that the child can and will make a

different choice tomorrow night when the same opportunity to wash up comes round again. This also reinforces the idea that there are no second chances at the time of the misbehavior.

*When they are finally in bed, the getting up and down begins. Brian suddenly remembers that he does have a homework paper that must be turned in tomorrow. He gets up to rummage around in his backpack to find it.*

It is too late to think of homework now. It is not all right to simply forget about responsibilities. Once Brian is in bed, he needs to stay in bed. He knew about his homework assignment earlier in the evening, but he chose to glue himself to the television set instead of completing his work. The consequences of his choices are that he will arrive at school tomorrow without the homework completed. This may mean disciplinary action of some kind, or it may mean he will receive a failing grade on that particular project. Whatever the consequences, they are his to accept as a result of his choice not to do his homework at an appropriate time.

His shading of the truth about not having any homework should be dealt with by the parents at a calm time. They should let him know what effect his lying had on them, that they felt hurt, angry, or disappointed. Parents should make a strong statement that they do not lie to their children and that they do not want their son to lie to them—that it damages family relationships. All of these types of statements should be delivered in a respectful but firm manner. It is important to talk *about* your feelings rather than act upon them.

*Kari remembers that there is a field trip tomorrow to a local museum all morning. The children are supposed to pack lunches to eat in the museum's outdoor picnic area.*

Kari, too, knew she had some special requirements for her school lunch for the coming day. She, like Brian, opted for television instead of preparing for the next day's events. The same rules should apply. Once Kari is in bed, she must remain there. It is too late for her suddenly to remember that a lunch must be packed for tomorrow.

The consequences for Kari are the same as with Brian. Because she didn't make the right choices about how she would spend her time earlier in the evening, she will go to school the following morning without her lunch. She will either have to miss out on the field trip or go without eating. Or, as a third consequence, Kari may decide to rise half an hour earlier in the morning so that she can prepare a lunch to take to school. Again, whichever of these three things happens, Kari is experiencing the consequences of her own decision to watch television and not take care of business.

*Mom rushes to fix Kari a lunch and help Brian finish his homework. Then she begins the process of getting them into bed all over again. When they balk, she loses her temper and threatens that she will not let Kari go on the field trip if they do not get to bed right now.*

*Dad hears the yelling and wades into the fray, telling the children they are distracting him. If he does not get his work done, he says, he will lose his job, and then they will all be homeless. The children giggle. They have heard this one before.*

This is business as usual for many families. The parents intervene when the children have made the wrong choices. They do not want the children to experience the consequences of bad choices. It is unthinkable to them that their son and daughter will go to school without the homework assignment or the proper lunch. Why?

There is a simple answer. When a child goes to school without his homework, when a child goes to school with no lunch for a field trip, parents feel their parenting will come under fire. They will be blamed, not the negligent children. After all, if they were good parents, the homework and the lunch would be there, even if it meant they had to take on the extra responsibility.

Parents are so afraid of appearing negligent that they routinely intervene and rescue their children from experiencing the consequences of poor choices and behaviors. If you are to successfully implement change within your family, you must be willing to give up this idea that others will judge you as bad parents when your children do not behave well.

If you do not give this fear up, you will simply continue rescuing your children until, finally, they are adults and you either no longer have the resources to rescue them or you are no longer around to do it. What do your children do then?

Rescuing children is a terrible disservice to them as people, for it teaches nothing about contribution, responsibility, or taking care of themselves. And the underlying message is a negative one. It goes something like, "Poor dear. You can't handle dealing with what you have done, so I'll handle it for you."

You are doing for them what they can and should be doing for themselves, and that is disrespectful to them. If someone were to do this to you, you might be insulted, yet you may be unaware that you are insulting your children by rescuing them. This dynamic is really about an adult's need to look good to others versus what is right for the child.

*Dad becomes even more incensed and gives Brian a swat, sending him off to bed crying. Kari dives beneath the covers before he can turn in her direction, but she is crying, too, by now.*

*Mom and dad end up having an argument about whether or not parents should spank children. By the time they stop arguing and dad finishes his work, it is very late, they are exhausted.*

This is the sad news about parents intervening to save their children. The resentment that builds when parents are acting from a place of anxiety and insecurity explodes at times like these and mom and dad end up battling over their children's behavior and being punitive instead of enjoying them.

This mother and father need to enlist their children's cooperation in fixing the evening meal, during which time, as a family, they can discuss the events of the day, as well as the requirements for the day to come. They can help children learn to be better organized.

Brian would most likely have been embarrassed and unhappy at school when it came time to turn in his assignment. Kari would probably have risen half an hour earlier to make her lunch so she could attend the field trip. Both of these children would have learned valuable lessons about taking responsibility for their needs instead of lounging about watching television while becoming more dependent on their parents.

We know what happens to children who grow up this way.

We all know adults we literally cannot stand to be around because they do not take responsibility for their poor behavior and thoughtless treatment of others. These people cannot have good relationships because they have no self-awareness and no concept of the give and take of living with other people.

Ask yourself if this is how you wish your children to function as adults. Of course the answer will be no. Therefore, you must prepare your children to live differently, to live responsibly, practically, and independently. That is your job as a parent, not helping do your child's homework so he will not be embarrassed or making last-minute lunches so your child can attend a school event.

The evening hours you spend getting your children through the laborious process of preparing for bed and actually going to sleep can be spent much more productively if you refuse to engage in nagging, threatening, complaining, or bullying your children to do what is right.

Instead, expect them to do the right things. Then, if and when your children do not rise to the occasion, let them experience all the consequences of their choices instead of bailing them out of their difficulties as a "permissive pal" type of parent would.

Most important, do not waste your evening fighting. You and your spouse have a right to a quiet, peaceful evening. Your children have a responsibility to the family to help make that happen. If they do not contribute and cooperate right away, simply continue on about your business and make your evening as pleasant as you can.

A crying child will soon stop crying and go to sleep, but not if you keep coming back to the bedroom every two minutes to either sympathize or threaten punishment. All you are doing in these instances is reinforcing the bad behavior, letting the child know that continued crying will get your attention.

You should let them know you appreciate their help and thoughtfulness, but do not praise them excessively for doing what is right. Instead, expect that they will take pride in their contribution to the family. They will develop an internal gauge whereby they can feel good about having places of importance in the group because they have done what is right. That is a good feeling. Why would you not want your children to experience it?

Remember that your parenting goals must be to instill this feeling of "belonging" in your children by encouraging positive behavior, not by lavishly praising it, but by respectfully acknowledging it. Sentences such as, "Thanks for your help," or "I notice you already brushed your teeth," go a long way with a child.

More important, you are creating an environment where there is no yelling, screaming, physical punishment, threatening, bribing, or slamming doors. When parents do not engage in these hysterics but do something else instead, children will sit up and take notice and positive change for the benefit of all will be well under way.

Now let's consider some very specific misbehaviors and how to deal with them using the techniques outlined thus far:

*Four-year-old Tyler gets up in the night and climbs into bed with his parents. He tells them he's too afraid to go back to sleep by himself and begs to be allowed to sleep with them.*

*When Tyler first started this behavior, mom and dad thought it was a phase that would pass. They allowed him*

*to stay and one of them would take him back to his own
bed once he'd fallen asleep.*

*Now, however, it has become a ritual almost every
night. In addition, Tyler wakes up once he's been taken
back to his own room and then goes back to his parents'
room demanding to be allowed to sleep with them again.*

*Everybody is losing sleep. What to do? The child is
afraid to sleep alone. Isn't it cruel to make him stay in his
room alone and afraid?*

The first time Tyler got up and came to mom and dad's room
because he was afraid may have been legitimate. However, because the parents did not deal with the problem that first time
it happened, it has now escalated.

This behavior is just like some of the examples that have already been discussed about children who get up over and over
again on the flimsiest of excuses in order to avoid going to sleep.
What they are doing is seeking attention and engaging in a
power struggle with their parents. What is more, they are winning.

When a child wants to sleep with mom and dad, the parents
need to make it clear to the child that they will not allow that to
happen. Mom and dad should firmly and respectfully escort the
child back to his or her room and, with confidence, say, "I know
you can handle this." Once you have gone beyond a simple
thing such as installing night-lights, you are not helping your
children grow and learn independence by catering to fears that
are being exploited to get parental attention.

A child who is taken back to bed and left there to go to sleep
may have one or two tearful tantrums before recognizing that
complaining about fears will not take him far when it comes to

getting to mom and dad. And, if you are the kind of parent who must soothe and placate and game-play with your child when he expresses something like fear of the dark, ask yourself why you would want to encourage your child to be fearful in the first place? Encouraging fears is what you are doing when you respond these ways.

The same strategy should be applied when children have nightmares. Once the child has been calmed, tucked back in, and assured that it was a nightmare, the parents can leave the room and let the child get back to sleep. By making more of this event than is necessary, a parent reinforces the idea that fear is a good thing because it gets a lot of attention and involvement from mom and dad. Suddenly, nightmares may become an every-night event. Why not? It worked the first time, didn't it?

It is always good, also, to let children know that you expect them to stay in their own beds and to get to sleep on time. That is one way they are contributing to the work of the family. Everyone needs sleep. Mom and dad have a right to a full night's sleep, too. Here is an example of the right way to handle a child who continues to get up out of bed:

*For about the last year, Matthew, age five, has developed the habit of getting up two and three times after he has been tucked into bed. He comes out of his bedroom, asking for water or food, asking what his parents are doing, saying he cannot sleep, or whatever comes to his mind.*

*Mom and dad have decided to do something different. They announce one night that they have been mishandling bedtime. They tell Matthew that from now on they will not talk with him after he goes to bed until the next morning. This statement is made with a loving but firm tone.*

*The test comes when Matthew gets up. What mom and dad do is completely ignore his presence. He is a "ghost" as far as they are concerned. When Matthew crawls over them on the couch, they say nothing and continue watching television or talking with each other as if he were not there.*

*If mom begins to get irritated, she can get up and go to the bathroom, draw a hot bath, and get in it in order not to show her reaction either verbally or physically. She need not sigh with exasperation or roll her eyes, or mutter under her breath. She merely gets up and leaves the room.*

*If dad is able to continue watching television without interacting with Matthew he should do so. If Matthew eventually falls asleep on the living room floor, they should throw a blanket over him and leave him there until the morning.*

*When Matthew wakes up, nothing is said. This is the hardest part because parents like to think that if they do not verbally point out what happened, the child will not "get it." Matthew's mom and dad know that this is not necessary for him to learn the lesson, and so they are respectful and say nothing.*

*Mom and dad may have to go through this process one or two more nights before Matthew completely gives up coming out to them after he has gone to bed.*

It is important to let the child learn about choices and consequences on his own. You take the proper action to teach, and then step back so the child can experience, think, and learn about the consequences of his actions.

Matthew learned from his parents' responses that he will get no attention when he gets up out of bed repeatedly, nor can he engage them in power struggles as they try to get him back to bed. In fact, they are so disengaged that he wakes up in the morning on the floor instead of in his bed. The message to the child is, "You can choose to sleep on the floor. That is your business. We're not involved once we put you to bed the first time. Our responsibilities are over. It is up to you."

It is not the end of the world if the child sleeps one or two nights on the floor. Just as it is not earthshaking for the child to miss a meal or go to school without homework. It will not harm the child to spend a night this way, though he may feel a bit stiff on getting up the next morning, as any of us would. It is usually something like that stiffness that tells us, "Uh-oh, I had better not do that again." That is the process of learning by experience. How else will your children learn to take care of themselves? Who will teach them about taking responsibility if you do not?

When children behave differently and get to sleep on time without disrupting the family by getting up over and over again, you need not praise their behavior. They are simply doing what they should do. However, once in a while you can let them know that you appreciate the contribution they make when they go to bed on time. Something like, "You sure have been cooperative about bedtime lately" will suffice. Remember the difference between lavish praise and simple acknowledgment.

Another important part of the "getting ready for bed" ritual is that it gives parents and children a special, private time together.

Children look forward to this and they will take charge of getting ready for bed in order to have time with mom and dad when they can discuss the day's events, read a story and talk about it, or talk over important family issues. This special time together really enhances relationships between parents and children. It is a time to feel important and loved in a very positive way.

Also, this special time of sharing between parents and children gives kids a much-needed opportunity to unwind from the stress of their days. And it is far more relaxing for children to talk for a little while with mom and dad at the end of the day than it is for them to sit in front of the television letting homework and other responsibilities pile up until the last minute. This kind of activity only serves to encourage children to get to bed late and to engage in a mad, anxiety-producing scramble to get ready for bed that is anything but relaxing.

Now let's write down a few quick ideas to help you gather your thoughts and prepare for changing the routine your children have come to regard as normal at bedtime.

## Bedtime Strategies

If I could change three things about my children's "getting ready for bed" routine each night they would be

1.

2.

3.

A good bedtime for my child(ren) is _____

To my children, "getting ready for bed" means:
- Bathing
- Brushing teeth
- Changing into pajamas
- _____
- _____
- _____
- _____

In order to be in bed and ready for sleep by this time, we need to begin bedtime preparations by _____

Right now, when my children do not get ready for bed I
_____
_____
_____

When my children do not want to get ready for bed I should
_____
_____
_____

List your goals for changing your children's bedtime routine:
_____
_____
_____

Think carefully about how you will change your responses to your children's behavior during the "getting ready for bed" routine. What patterns are now in place? What would you like to change? How will you alter your responses in order to promote the positive changes you are looking for?

These changes will not happen overnight. You must plan and develop strategies to create new, positive habits for you and your children. You will succeed, however, if you are respectful, consistent, and careful to follow through with all consequences.

Here is an example of what one mother did when confronted with small children who refused to get out of the bathtub and into their pajamas:

*Mom bathes her children, ages three, four, and five together each evening. It is usually difficult for her to get them into the tub, but tonight she is having trouble getting them out.*

*She says, "Okay, time to get out and get ready for bed." They whine and refuse to move. She is exhausted and does not want to have to lift them out as she ordinarily would with a great deal of anger. So she says, "Okay," and walks out the door, shutting off the light as she goes.*

*Staying close by the bathroom, she waits. The children come out soon afterward. They have gotten out of the tub on their own, dried off, and are now looking for their pajamas. She assists them as needed, without comment, and they are soon ready for bed.*

*She was shocked when, the next night, she bathed the children and they got right out of the tub when she asked them to.*

This mom did a lot of things right:

- She did not engage in a power struggle by physically removing them.
- She waited and watched, giving them the opportunity to take care of themselves.
- She was helpful with the pajamas as needed, indicating that she had let the incident go.
- She did not lecture, yell, threaten, or punish the children when they did not do as she asked.
- She did not bribe or resort to whining.
- She let them choose to stay in the tub and experience the consequences of that choice.

Common sense and a little careful planning on how to deal with situations that will arise can go a long way toward changing your family's evening routines. Bedtimes need not be battlegrounds. Change them into peaceful, happy times that you and your children can enjoy together.

## This Chapter in a Nutshell

- Preparing for bed begins when you arrive home at the end of the day, not fifteen minutes before children are to be asleep.
- Set firm bedtimes for your children and stick to them.
- Use calm, respectful language at all times, and follow through with logical consequences.
- Do not engage in verbal or physical battles with your children about bedtime.
- Do not "rescue" your children when they want more food,

multiple drinks of water, more bedtime stories, or other such things children use as excuses to delay going to sleep.

- Offer children a small number of choices such as, "Would you like to wash your face or shall I do it for you?" Then follow through calmly and respectfully if the children do not begin to accomplish the tasks themselves.

- Allow children to learn about responsibility and independence by getting ready for bed on their own and by experiencing the consequences of their misbehavior without parents "rescuing" them.

- Do not let homework become a nightly battle. Change your attitudes about it. Examine your motives for getting overinvested in your child's assignments.

- All members of the family deserve a quiet, pleasant evening free from battles, anxiety, threats, last-minute emergencies, and hysterics.

- Children can learn that contributing to the family and establishing their places of importance in the group are accomplished by taking care of homework, preparing for the next day, getting ready for bed on time, and getting to sleep so they are rested for the twenty-four hours ahead.

# 4.

# Getting Up: A Gracious Good Morning to You

*"Rhythm (or regularity) is a premise of life. The earlier the child is confronted with rhythm, the better."*
—RUDOLF DREIKURS

It should be very clear to you by now that the way a day progresses, winds down, and builds toward the next morning is a continuum of activity with interlocking parts. No hours in the day are isolated events or incidents that do not carry forward into the rhythm of your life and your children's lives. That is why it is so important to look at the behavior in your family and begin to analyze the patterns that repeat themselves over and over again throughout a twenty-four-hour period.

By the time you reach this chapter, you should also see that this book promotes two essential ideas that parents may embrace in order to bring order and peace to all the day-to-day processes involving the family. First, one of the most important things you can do for your children is provide them with a sense of belonging within the family.

You have to have faith that your children want to cooperate and contribute but are misbehaving in a misguided bid for attention and power. Your basic belief must be that your children want to do the right thing. You need to have high expectations that they will use positive means to belong after you allow them to do so. You are teaching your children to care for others and to demonstrate that caring by taking on responsibilities that help family life run smoothly.

Second, you are doing your children a great service by encouraging them to use and build skills that will serve them well. Cooperation, contribution, care, and thoughtfulness are attributes that they will use in every aspect of their adult lives. These are the essential tools of emotional, intellectual, and physical survival that we all need in order to master the complexities of our world.

Letting your children make choices and experience consequences is essential to the process of learning and growing that will culminate in adulthood. Where will they learn about responsibility, respect, and productivity if not from their parents?

Changing your children's behavior means first assessing and changing your reactions and responses. Learn positive ways of interacting with your family, which, in turn, can be used in every arena of your own life. The bonus of helping your children learn productive behavior is that you help yourself. With these ideas in mind, we can begin to tackle the ways in which your days begin. See if the following scenario sounds familiar:

*Eight-year-old Tamara's mother wakes her in plenty of time for breakfast, dressing, and getting her school supplies ready to go. The only hitch is that Tamara does not get up.*

*After waking her daughter, mom goes off to get ready for work, but she knows she will have to stop what she is doing and come back three or four times to get the child out of bed. This constant repetition results in a significant loss of time for everyone.*

*Mom finally prevails, and Tamara gets out of bed and goes to the bathroom. However, just getting the child up and out of bed does not mean the problem is resolved. In fact, the conflicts of the morning are just beginning.*

*Now mom must tell Tamara what to wear and what to eat for breakfast, and she must also prepare the child's lunch and get her school supplies ready and in her backpack.*

*Tamara fights every step of the way. She wants to wear the blue dress, not the red one. She wants different socks. She does not want another peanut butter sandwich in her lunch. She is unable to find the homework she did last night.*

*Dad is getting impatient. He has to be out of the house at a precise time in order to make a substantial commute and get to work on time. He has fixed breakfast, but nobody is there to eat it. Mom and Tamara are arguing in the bedroom. He weighs in by yelling that they had better hurry up because he cannot afford to be late again.*

*On and on it goes until the mad dash out the door with everyone frantic about being late and dad so angry that he has no business getting behind the wheel of a car.*

These morning battles are repeated daily in homes across the country. Parents battle with powerful, often overtired, children who want to stay in bed and sleep, even though they know they must get up and go to school. The parents have their own jobs to get to, but it is their responsibility to see that the child gets up and gets to school on time. At least that is what we think, right?

As has been mentioned before, many parents are afraid of what others will think of them or that they will be considered negligent if their children are not well dressed, well fed, and organized when they arrive at school. What is more, many parents feel they are alone in these battles with their children. They do not realize that in their neighbors' homes the same struggles are being played out. Worse yet, they do not realize that this nerve-wracking cycle can end with some careful planning on their part. These parents are currently buying into the notion that somehow this chaos is a force of nature that cannot be changed. They are abdicating their responsibilities as leaders of the family. If the parents have given up, what do you think the children are feeling?

No parent wants repeatedly to go through this exhausting routine every morning, especially with an eight-hour (or longer!) workday ahead of them. What if the mom and dad described in the previous scenario could wave a magic wand and change the morning battles? Their morning might be very different, going something like this:

*Mom and dad rise at their normal time and begin to pre-pare for the day. They only have to worry about getting themselves up and going because they know that Tamara is capable of getting herself out of bed and ready for school.*

*Tamara's alarm clock rings, and she gets out of bed and walks over to her dresser to shut it off. She washes her face, combs her hair, and then dresses herself in the outfit she has chosen the night before.*

*Having done that, she collects her backpack, which she has packed the night before with her homework and the other items she must take with her to school.*

*Tamara then joins her parents in the kitchen because she knows mom and dad are depending upon her to set the table and put out the cereal, milk, and fruit for everyone.*

*In the meantime, mom and dad have dressed, collected the things they must take to work, and are in the kitchen preparing coffee and talking about their day's plans. While Tamara does her job, she joins in and discusses what kinds of things she will be doing throughout the day.*

*After they have all eaten, mom quickly cleans up the breakfast clutter while dad and Tamara make lunches to take along. The time taken to accomplish all this is much less than the time this family would normally have spent on their morning's activities.*

*In the past, the time needed for this small family to get ready and out the door was nearly doubled because of the dawdling, nagging, and disorganization that had been their usual routine.*

*Now anger and haste have been replaced by calm, peaceful order as each member of the family goes about the tasks he or she has agreed to do. Cooperation, contribution, and responsibility have replaced the chaos of the past.*

Unrealistic? A dream that will never happen? My kids? Yes, your children can and, most important, probably want to, behave this way. Chaotic mornings and battles over every little thing are not pleasant for them, either. You know how you feel after squabbling your way out the door. Why would your children feel any better about the situation than you do?

Parents can choose to change the ways they interact with their children and make this positive scenario a reality in their homes. It does not require loud voices, physical intimidation, wheedling, cajoling, or making promises of any kind. Nor does it take a magic wand to transform your mornings from chaos to cooperation.

It does, however, take some planning, some patience, and some pattern-breaking strategies to lay the groundwork for mornings that go smoothly, pleasantly, and efficiently for all parties in the household. And it is up to you as the parents to start this ball rolling.

One of the most important things you must do is make a commitment to changing your family's disruptive cycle by first changing your responses to the battles. Review the kind of parent you are in the morning.

If you are a parent who is acting the "boss," you will probably find yourself doing tyrannical things. Some parents are guilty of rousting children out of bed at an appointed time and then coming back in to yell and nag when the child does not get right up.

Then, when the yelling and nagging do not get the desired results, these parents take drastic measures such as yanking the covers off the bed, threatening dire punishments, and physically pulling the child out of bed. Some parents even go so far as to throw cold water in the faces of their sleeping children. Can you imagine waking up to that? What kinds of feelings of cooperation and contribution will this disrespectful treatment bring forth?

As Oscar Christensen says, "Always treat your child the way you would your best friend." If your best friend were sleeping over, would you ever do any of these things to wake that person up? And, if not, then why do you believe it is all right to treat your children this way? How much more respectful it is simply to go about your own business and let them be late and face the consequences.

If you are an indulgent parent who is used to rescuing, you may wake your child gently over and over again. You may repeatedly stop yourself in the middle of your own morning routine to go back to the child's room and hover, prodding, bribing, and pleading with the child to "help mommy" by getting up. You may promise exotic treats such as ice cream for breakfast or extra money for a lunchtime treat.

No matter which of these approaches most closely mirrors the one you now use, the plain fact is that neither of them works. The child will continue to sleep in, dawdle, refuse to get dressed, poke around at breakfast food, and find what seems like a hundred other little ways to annoy you and hold up your progress. The child is experiencing a heady sense of power by holding mom and dad captive every morning. No one can leave the house until the child is ready to do so.

That is a great deal of importance for a child to experience. However, as has already been pointed out, it is the wrong kind of importance, for it disrupts the family and teaches nothing about cooperation and caring. No one feels good, even though the child may experience a short-term feeling of winning the power struggle with mom and dad.

All of that attention may serve to bolster the child's feelings of power over others for a short time, but, since the child is not engaged in positive behaviors, the long-term effects on the child are anything but bolstering. And when a child who gains attention this way takes this same behavior to school or to the social world outside the home, he is often not successful or well liked by others. He will suffer from this misplaced feeling of power and importance because it is a mistaken way of belonging. He is working against others instead of for and with others.

Needless to say, the child is learning all the wrong things when it comes to human relationships. He or she may not have learned what is needed to become a whole and healthy adult but will carry misbehavior into adulthood, unable to cooperate with other people, contribute to society, or form lasting, caring relationships. The earlier parents begin working as teachers who wish their children to be happy, productive members of the family, the easier it is to teach the lessons that make for happy, productive members of society.

To begin teaching these lessons, parents must choose a third alternative. They must choose to become respectful, thoughtful parents who have outlined a plan of action they will use to change the chaotic morning ritual.

It is your job as the family leader to decide what time everyone must be up and out of bed in order to get out of the house on time. And it is also part of your job to make a plan for which family members will do specific morning chores. It certainly helps to ask for your children's input when you put the plan together, however. What they have to say can be very valuable and eye-opening. And when they have contributed to thinking about the way the morning will go, they generally are more enthusiastic about doing their parts.

Once you provide your children with the knowledge and the tools they will need to accomplish their particular contributions to the morning plan, you are done. Other than paying close attention to your own behavior so that your responses are what they should be, you may now step back and let your children take responsibility for morning activities.

It is surprising to realize that many parents have never considered simply outlining a morning plan and expecting that their children will be willing to take part in it. You may be among those who have been so caught up in the daily strife of your family's life that you have not considered alternatives.

Perhaps you have not believed that change is possible. But begin now to consider seriously the potential for change within your own family, and focus first of all on changing yourself and your responses.

It is important to stress once again that having high expectations and faith in your children is an important part of parenting as teachers instead of as "bosses" or "permissive pals." But have some faith in yourself, as well. You will not succeed overnight, but you will begin to see results fairly quickly. You have two challenges.

The first is to have faith that if you, as a parent, are consistent and continue to expect your children to take responsibility for their morning routine, they will rise to the occasion. Your second challenge is to follow through with the logical consequences that provide lessons for your children so that next time they will make better choices.

Here's how you do it:

- Be calm, respectful, and firm as you go about your morning routine.
- Buy an alarm clock for each child. Even a young child can learn to set and use it.
- Place the alarm clock on the other side of the bedroom so

that the child has to physically rise from the bed each morning to shut it off.

- Do not check on the child in the morning. Expect that the child will get up, shut off the alarm, and get ready for school.
- If the child is not ready and has not eaten breakfast when it is time to leave, he or she goes to school "as is" without comment from you.
- Repeat this routine as often as needed, following through with consequences each morning.
- Do not talk about or explain your actions, and do not give second chances when the child promises to behave once consequences begin to unfold.
- If you talk at all, express faith by saying, "Maybe tomorrow morning will go better."

On the surface this may sound like an overly simple approach to organizing your morning's activities. However, like all the suggestions made in this book, changing your morning routine depends on you and your family agreeing on procedures for those morning activities and establishing consequences for those who do not take responsibility for getting up and getting dressed.

In order to give up attempts to control, you must dramatically alter your parental inclination to nag, push, lecture, and otherwise "motivate" your child to get ready for the day. You must rethink your role as a parent and realize that bad behavior on your part (yelling, threatening, bribing, and so on) will not result in good behavior from your children.

And it does not help you to get angry or frustrated as each day begins. Keeping your cool is important to the way you manage stress. Here is an example of how one mother kept her cool during the familiar morning "clothes wars":

> *Ten-year-old Stephanie decides that she does not want to wear to school today what she and mother picked out last night. Mother hears her griping and whining and stomping around in her room. Time is passing and mother worries that they will all be late.*
>
> *She goes into Stephanie's room and asks her what the problem is. Stephanie protests that she wants to wear her halter-top and shorts since it is warm outside. Mother disagrees and tells Stephanie that she does not approve of that kind of dress for school.*
>
> *Stephanie begins to yell and scream that it is her life and she should be able to decide what she wants to wear. She says all her friends dress this way. Her mother does not engage in that argument with her, nor does she fall back on the time-worn parental response of pointing out, "And would you jump off the bridge if all your friends did?"*
>
> *Instead, mother offers Stephanie a choice. She holds up two outfits and says, "Would you like to choose one of these to wear, or would you like for me to choose?"*
>
> *When Stephanie continues to complain, mom stands by neutrally. She does not get irritated or impatient. She simply takes Stephanie's refusal to pick an outfit as an indication of her choice to let her mom make the selection.*
>
> *Mom leaves one outfit on the bed and exits the room. If Stephanie is not dressed in the outfit by the time everyone is ready to leave, mom may provide her an overcoat but otherwise takes her to school "as is."*

If Stephanie is very powerful and escalates by putting on the halter-top and shorts and coming to the door dressed that way, mom is ready. She has thought of several options. She could take Stephanie to her grandmother's house for the day. She could call in a sitter to stay with her. Her neighbor is at home and could be called on. In this case, mom asks her neighbor to please have Stephanie over for the day because she cannot go to school the way she is dressed.

Do not worry that you will have to go through this whole process every day. At the most, you will only need to do this one or two mornings for your child to learn the lesson. If Stephanie rushes and changes her halter-top for the outfit mom has picked out, it is not good enough. The consequences take place regardless of her last-minute decision to cooperate.

Giving up control also means that you must relinquish your expectation that your children cannot perform these simple tasks on their own, and that without you, the parent, intervening every step of the way, the child can not possibly be ready to leave at the appropriate time. You must make a complete turnaround in the way you view your child and your role as the parent and teacher of that child.

Here is where it becomes so important for you to have faith in your children, for, as Dreikurs says, "If we are to have better children, parents must become better educators." This principle must be foremost in the minds of parents if they are to begin achieving change within the family. When you step back and let children do things for themselves, accept responsibility, and deal with consequences, you are truly teaching.

This is a good example that takes us back to our original guiding principle that parents must firmly commit themselves to the idea that in order to change their children's behavior they must first change their own responses and reactions. It is essential that parents begin their work by shifting the focus to themselves and seeing themselves in a new light. The parent who gives up control in the morning is changing his responses and then waiting to see what effect those changes will have on the family.

A key Adlerian idea is that you must learn to manage yourself instead of trying to manage your children. In order to manage yourself, you must know yourself and understand your behaviors and their effects very well. This is how you gain the courage to step back and let your children be responsible for things.

It is possible to break a cycle of perpetual conflict, unproductive use of time, and disorganization. The worst part of this kind of cycle is that it deprives parents and children of the enjoyment of each other that should be the natural outgrowth of the parent-child relationship. Imagine replacing antagonism with enjoyment, and accept that you can do this. These are the kinds of things that are in your control.

It is not enough to think about what style of parenting you have adopted with your own children. You may already have identified yourself as a "boss" or a "permissive pal," but now consider why those parenting techniques seem acceptable to you.

Are these the behaviors your own parents modeled? Or are you operating in opposition to your parents' behaviors, choosing to be a "permissive pal" because your parents were the autocratic bosses?

The problems you are experiencing each morning may be the result of parenting behaviors you have never fully examined. For example, on the whole, there is too much parental involvement and talking in the process of getting the child up and ready each day. Here is how one mom intervened and rescued her son repeatedly:

*Sixteen-year-old Ian sleeps in several mornings each week. He does not respond to his parents' pleas to get up. He is late for school regularly.*

*Dad can leave for work on time, but mother, who doesn't work outside the home, has to contend with Ian's lateness almost every day. She has made a habit of waking him up over and over until finally he gets out of bed and gets dressed.*

*By this time, he has missed most of first period, and he knows he will be in trouble without some help from mom. Mom does not want his grades to suffer or for him to be labeled a "problem" at school, so she gets on the phone on the mornings he is late and calls the school.*

*She tells the attendance officer that her son is on his way and was sick this morning. She asks for an "excused absence." Mom knows this is wrong and that she is modeling poor behavior, but she has not really thought this whole process through. She tells herself she is protecting her son and helping him. He is a good boy, but he just cannot get up on time.*

*They go along this way for several weeks, but one day, mother has an early-morning appointment of her own and cannot be there to get Ian up and call the school for him. He sleeps in, and, without mom there to pave the way, decides he will just stay home all day.*

*When mom returns, Ian is playing video games. He tells her he is staying home all day and will need a note from her saying that he was sick. Mom realizes this problem is getting out of hand. Now her son is missing school and asking her to lie.*

*She decides to change her ways. She tells Ian she will*

*not write the note and that she feels she has been mishandling this whole situation. He must get himself up on time and out the door without her intervention from here on out.*

*The next morning, Ian sleeps in as usual. However, true to her word, mom does not wake him. In fact, she does not check on him at all. The result is that Ian oversleeps by an hour. He gets up, frantically dresses, goes to his mother and says, "You didn't wake me up!" Then he demands that she call the school with an excuse since it was her fault he did not get up.*

*Mom picks up the phone and calls. But Ian hears her say, "My son is on his way. He is late because he chose not to get up this morning. This is not an excused absence."*

*Much to mom's surprise the attendance officer is shocked and grateful for her honesty. She tells mom, "You are the first parent in a long time who has told the truth about why your child is late." Mom feels good and strong.*

*When her son, furious and upset, yells and complains, she stays neutral, looking at him as if she does not understand what the problem is. Ian gives up ranting and goes to school. He spends an afternoon in study hall making up the time.*

Many parents may feel they are protecting their children when they are really helping them develop some very bad habits. The underlying message to your child is a very demoralizing one. It is, "I cannot count on you to do what is required, so I have to rescue you. You cannot handle it."

All you have to do is think about how you would feel if your boss or friends held this belief about you and intervened and rescued you at every turn. What if people routinely took away your work projects because they did not think you could do them on your own? You would resent them, and, furthermore, you would begin to feel bad about yourself and your abilities. Why should things be any different for your children when you feel the need to protect and rescue them?

Parents who do this kind of intervening may feel that children, especially younger ones, do not have the knowledge or skills to get up and get ready for the day, but where does this assessment of a child's abilities come from? Is parental involvement simply a habit that, once adopted, has become so much a part of the morning routine that no one even thinks about it any longer?

How is the child to understand and appreciate the positive results of doing things for himself if the parents are always fussing, prompting, and intervening? Imagine how you would feel if, every morning, you were treated this way. It would be demoralizing and not a little humiliating. You would probably begin to engage in attention-getting power struggles yourself, if only to assert your independence and feel as if you had some importance in the process.

Remember that children need to experience the positive consequences of the choices they make, as well as the not so positive ones that result from mistakes in their judgment. Many good things happen when your children cooperate and help out.

When you allow your child to do these tasks without your interference, you are allowing plenty of room for such positive consequences as feelings of accomplishment, appreciation of creating well-organized routines, and the knowledge that he or she has helped the family get off on the right foot each morning. Here are some ideas you can use as you begin to plan how you would like your morning routine to change.

Purchase an alarm clock for each child who is old enough to learn to use it. The immediate benefit, of course, is that parents no longer take on the responsibility of waking the children each morning. You should purchase alarm clocks for younger children, too, but you will want to teach them how to turn it on at night and off in the morning when they get up.

But there are more important messages being communicated to the children. Parents are encouraging their children to take an active role in beginning their day. In addition, parents are demonstrating faith in their children's ability to take on responsibility and follow through with their obligations.

The children are learning some very elementary skills related to taking good care of themselves. It is a source of pride for a child to turn on the alarm clock each night and then get up on his or her own when it rings in the morning. One of the problems children experience in growing up and accepting responsibility is dealing with parental overinvolvement.

If you wish to change your family's morning dynamic, you need to give up a lot of that unnecessary involvement. When you remove yourself from the equation, you have essentially put the child in charge of orchestrating his own morning routine. This is a positive way of empowering a child within the family. You follow through with this idea by going about your business.

There is no reason to check up on the child and make sure he has gotten up on time. Again, you are demonstrating faith in your child and faith in the importance of the child's behavior. You are letting your child experience some very positive consequences of good behavior.

Perhaps, the first morning you attempt this change, everything will not go smoothly. Your faith may be tested, but that is no reason to fall back on your old patterns of nagging, threaten-

ing, or bribing. Your child may not get it right the first time.
Take heart. There is a new morning every day, and you will see
results if you persist in your expectations that your child will
take the initiative and do what must be done. That is what is
meant by "follow through," and you must implement logical
consequences as many times as is necessary to facilitate changes.

If the child is not ready on time, that is no reason not to leave
the house as scheduled. You should not be late because your child
has not done what needs to be done in the allotted time. Your child
must go to school "as is" and, if breakfast has not been eaten, be
hungry until lunchtime. If this seems harsh to you, remember that
you are doing nothing more than allowing your child to experience
the consequences of his or her morning behaviors.

Many children use the morning as a time to engage in power
struggles such as sleeping in, dawdling, or refusing to eat breakfast. The child knows what must be done and why. The more
you lecture and explain, the less you are acknowledging your
child's ability to understand, and thus do, what is needed.

If mother and father must leave the house by 7:30 A.M. in order to drop the kids at school and get to work on time, then the
children must also be ready to leave at that time. Thinking of
others is a vital part of contributing to the family. A child who
does not help the family meet its morning schedule is a child
who is finding his significance working against the common
good of his family.

If the child has to go to school without having eaten breakfast or without the right outfit or homework, that child experiences some very real consequences that he or she will not want
to repeat. Your job as a parent is to remain calm and respectful
as you exit the house at the appointed time.

The only thing a parent should say is something like, "Maybe things will go better tomorrow." And remember that this is said calmly and without a sarcastic, confrontational, or lecturing tone. You are not punishing the child by taking him to school "as is." You are meeting the schedule that has been established by you and your children, and you are simply following through with the logical consequences of the child's behavior.

To see this through correctly, you need not have involved yourself in the child's morning routine at all. Remember that too much misplaced parental involvement is often at the heart of the child's misbehavior.

In the past, you may have wasted a great deal of time coaxing your child out of bed, arguing about what clothes should be worn, hunting frantically for shoes and homework, and hurriedly stuffing sandwiches into bags for lunch. Your child may have pushed every parental button you have by playing at the computer or turning on the television when he or she should have been dressing or eating breakfast.

Once again, as a consequence for this kind of misbehavior (watching television, playing games) you can unplug or remove the television set. Games are easily put away and given back when you decide to do so.

The cycle of conflict, chaos, and hurry is a terrible way to begin each day. Many parents do not understand the part they play in these chaotic mornings, beginning with the simple, pervasive assumption that it is their job to wake their children up each morning.

Parents need to take the time to sit down with their children and discuss what is expected of them. Jointly, they can set out the timetable that must be met each morning. Input should be elicited from the children when making up the timetable. This gives them an investment in the process, and it is a respectful way to treat them.

Make a timeline of the things that you and your family need to accomplish each morning. The timeline may look something like this:

| 6:00 A.M. | Mom and dad up, getting ready |
| 6:15 A.M. | Kids up, getting ready |
| 6:45 A.M. | Kids set out breakfast items |
| 7:00 A.M. | Everybody eats |
| 7:15 A.M. | Dad cleans up<br>Mom makes lunches<br>Kids get backpacks |
| 7:30 A.M. | Everybody leaves the house |

It is not easy to coordinate schedules for a busy family, and you may be thinking this timeline looks too simple since you may exercise, walk the dog, or do other activities in the morning prior to leaving the house. But, individual activities aside, consider what you may currently be going through every morning. You probably have no timeline at all, no projected goals for how or when your family might actually accomplish that miracle of leaving the house on time.

You may never have thought about how to organize your morning, assign chores, and lay out a pattern for getting ready. When you do not put order into your day, there is no way for it to run smoothly. Your present timeline, or what there is of it, may look something like this:

| | |
|---|---|
| 6:00 A.M. | Mom and dad up, getting ready |
| 6:15 A.M. | Mom and dad wake kids, leave them to continue getting ready |
| 6:25 A.M. | Mom and dad wake kids again and get them up after repeated attempts |
| 6:30 A.M. | Kids finally up |
| 7:00 A.M. | Mom and dad tell kids to dress. Kids cannot choose clothes, dawdle, wander into kitchen in their pajamas |
| 7:30 A.M. | Kids dressed, but no time for breakfast, can't find homework |
| 7:40 A.M. | No lunches are made, kids must be given lunch money |
| 7:45 A.M. (or later!) | Kids finally dressed but late, frazzled, hungry when they at last get out the door |

It may take several days of letting your children experience the consequences of their morning behaviors. You must cultivate patience, calmness, firmness, and an unwavering conviction that you are doing the right thing and that the first timeline is something your family can and will achieve.

Because these are new concepts for your family, and because change does not happen overnight (no matter how much we might wish it!), you should be prepared for the usual sleeping in, dawdling, and lack of organization you have witnessed in the past. What is different this time is your response. You will not become angry, nor will you interfere or involve yourself in your children's misbehaviors.

Many times parents are surprised that merely announcing the new process is all that is needed and that the children do not challenge the changes parents are making.

*Mom tells her children, ages twelve, ten, and eight, that she has been mishandling the morning routine. From now on, they will be responsible for getting themselves up and ready every morning. She also adds that they are old enough to fix their own lunches and make sure they have everything they need for school.*

*She tells them she has made a list of all the things that need to be done each morning, and she needs their help. She asks them to volunteer for one chore each.*

*Her children protest that they are afraid they will not remember to do all this, but mom responds with encouragement, saying, "I know you can handle it." Once she does not engage in explaining herself or responding to their protests, the children each pick a chore.*

*The next morning, mom finds the children get up and do everything she has asked. She is shocked and pleased at how her plan worked.*

This mother is successful for many reasons. First of all, she admitted her own imperfections. She spoke respectfully, without emoting, and she asked for her children's help instead of demanding that they do something because she told them to do it. It is true that very powerful children who have a long history of winning power struggles will not likely respond this well this quickly. However, many children relish the opportunity to help mom and like taking responsibility. If you are dealing with very powerful children, the philosophy and techniques remain the same. They just take longer, and that requires you to continue to be patient and to follow through.

You will do only what you need to do for yourself, and, at the appointed time, you will gather everyone up and leave the house. If little Rose is wearing her dress over her pajama bottoms, then that is how she will go to school. If Jeremy cannot find his homework, he will leave without it. If neither child has time to eat, they will leave without breakfast and be hungry.

Rose will go to school dressed as she has chosen to dress. Jeremy will have no homework when his teacher asks for it. Having experienced these things, Jeremy and Rose will begin to think about making different choices for themselves the following morning. By continuing to follow through with your plan, you will begin to see results. Remember, you must be patient and consistent.

You are not lecturing, nagging, saying, "I told you so," or using your parental authority to muscle your children out the door. Rather, you are sticking to a plan and you are allowing your children to experience the logical consequences of their morning choices.

If tomorrow your children do not do the right thing, you state again, but only once, that you believe "things will go better the next day." It is damaging to retract your belief in the child based on the child's mistakes that day because to do so undermines what you are building. Become a "cockeyed optimist" where your kids are concerned! Do not give up. Your job as the family leader is to keep teaching and training for as long as it takes. Remember, however, that change usually occurs after one or two mornings of follow-through.

You are teaching through example, also, for you are fully dressed, have eaten breakfast, and have all the materials you need with you for work when you leave the house. The children have the ability to be just as pulled together each morning, and you are helping them learn about their own abilities when you follow through.

You need to give up the idea that without your involvement, they cannot get through these simple tasks. Remember, you are not asking them to do the impossible. You are expecting that they will accomplish simple, helpful tasks, get into the car, and be ready to go. That will help the entire family get off to a good start each morning. But what about when this does not happen?

*Ten-year-old Danny and his four-year-old sister Emma are in the car with seat belts on waiting for mother to drive them to school. As mom approaches the car, Emma begins to whine that the purple bunny she has with her is not the right stuffed animal to take to day care.*

*Mom leans in and asks her why she is crying. Big brother in the front seat is beginning to roll his eyes because he knows that Emma is starting the process of working her mother over. Too bad mom does not get it.*

*Emma whimpers that she wants the pink dinosaur instead of the purple bunny. Mom sighs, and then she goes back in the house. She comes back out with the pink dinosaur only to find that what Emma really wants is the chickie. Mom, of course, is getting irritated. However, in order to try and get this show on the road she goes back in the house to get the chickie.*

*Can you guess what happens next? Yes, mom comes back with a yellow chickie, only to find that Emma wanted the green one, not the yellow one. Mom loses it. She yells, gets in the car, slams the door and says, "I'm not putting up with this anymore!" Danny snickers as he looks out the window.*

Round one to Emma. Too bad mom did not know that the purpose of Emma's whining and indecision was to put her mother in her service. This child believes that she is only important if she is the center of attention. She is successful in meeting her mistaken goals of belonging this way. Mom is clueless. She is taking the child's requests at face value and seems to have no interior gauge to help her know when her child is shamelessly manipulating her.

This mom is not alone. Many well-meaning parents just do not get it. They do not know the difference between genuine requests and the kinds of requests that only have to do with demonstrating power. Here is another example of this same kind of manipulation, but this time, dad gets it right.

*Five-year-old Michael is ready to go. Dad helps him into the car, belts him in, and gets behind the wheel. Dad drives about half a block when Michael begins to wail. Oh, no. The boy just realized he is not wearing his blue jacket. That is the one he likes best. Where is it? Dad has to go back right away. Michael cannot go to school without it.*

*Dad has heard it all before. He sighs in exasperation. The first few times Michael tried this ploy, dad would go back and get the jacket, hat, T-shirt, shoes, toy—whatever the child had to have in order to live through the day. Then dad wised up.*

*This time, he is determined to ignore the behavior and go on driving. It is not easy, but dad steels himself and pretends the child is not wailing right beside him.*

*He may turn on the radio and listen to some music, or he may just start singing himself. He could also start talking about other things such as a big truck on the highway and see if Michael will drop the jacket issue.*

*Whatever he does, this dad has decided enough is enough. He does not give in and go back for the jacket. He does not even discuss it or try and placate the child. He assumes his child will pull it together, even if he has to repeat this process for two or three more days.*

*He has faith that Michael can learn either to have the object with him when he leaves or to let the matter drop in the spirit of cooperation. Whichever choice Michael makes, it is his.*

This dad has finally learned that he will be late for work every day unless he takes steps to make sure he does not let his child's bids for attention get the better of his morning schedule. Dad has created a plan that will get them out the door on time, and he is keeping to that plan regardless of Michael's attempts to sabotage it. He knows that an organized morning schedule is important to the whole family, and he knows he is modeling responsible behavior for his son when he keeps things moving and does not get sidetracked by Michael's demands.

Once you have created your morning plan, you need to make doubly sure that you do not let your child's bids for attention through manipulation interfere with your objectives. Your child may have gotten over dawdling over her cereal, but she may try another power play when you are in the car and ready to go. Prepare for this kind of behavior, be ready to keep going, and have faith that your child will soon give up misbehaving this way too.

Planning is the most important part of achieving your goals, and keeping to your plan is essential. With the timeline examples used earlier firmly in mind, take a moment to create your own family timeline that you will use in the morning. Consider the activities listed below and choose the ones your family must accomplish before leaving the house. Then estimate how much time each activity will take.

Use these estimated times to determine how early you and your children must wake up and when you must leave the house to be on time. The activities listed are guides, but you should be specific and create your own list of activities that pertain to your family. Spend some time thinking of all the things you and your children must do each step of the way. You may be surprised at how long your list will become. Ask for your children's help in coming up with the list. This can be fun. You may find it helpful to create timelines like this one for your afternoons and evenings as well.

*The tasks my family must accomplish each morning before leaving the house are:*

1. Wake up

2. Exercise

3. Bathe/dress/get completely ready for school or work

4. Walk dog

5. Gather items that must be taken when family leaves house

6. Prepare breakfast

7. Eat

8. Brush teeth

9. Clean up after breakfast

10. Pack lunches

11. Make beds

12. Leave the house on time

13. Other _____

*My family's timeline is:*

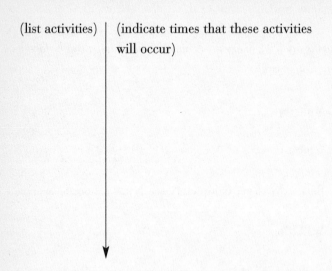

(list activities)     (indicate times that these activities
will occur)

Are you more comfortable making the next day's lunches in the evening rather than trying to make them in the morning before you leave? Then do it that way. It is often easier on everyone in the morning if several things have been done in preparation the night before. For example, it helps if children choose tomorrow's clothes the night before or bathe or shower so as to shorten the morning routine.

Your family may have helpful patterns of activity that you want to incorporate into your plans. If, for instance, your children come in from school and immediately do their homework before dinner, then it is logical to have them pack their backpacks and have everything ready to go for the next morning as soon as they have finished their schoolwork.

The key is to establish a new, more harmonious and productive routine, but we do not want to throw out the baby with the bathwater. If there are things that work for you, use them. Build your timelines around them. You will most probably find yourself adjusting the times and activities as you begin to make the preliminary changes.

You may redo, readjust, and redraw your timelines until you feel you have created a plan that works. Allow yourself ample time to do the tasks you set out on the timeline. When your children provide input, simply say, "Thanks, those are good ideas."

The timeline really only helps you as a way to formulate a plan, get organized, and create a new pattern of behavior to replace the old patterns of chaos, disruption, and disorganization. Remember that you cannot simply do away with your children's misbehavior without giving some thought to what will replace the old patterns. You must provide alternatives, and part of that has to do with letting children experience choices and consequences. The other part is encouraging them to shoulder more of the tasks themselves.

One important thing that has been mentioned before is that you must have high expectations for your children while at the same time planning how you will respond if they do not meet those high expectations for a few days. If you have carefully thought out, even rehearsed, some situations in your own mind, you will be ready with correct responses, and there is more likelihood that you will follow through with the consequences you have already considered.

In addition, you will have made a commitment to the training process, realizing that you will have to invest some time and patience in teaching your children how to do things in new ways. High expectations are important, but you must also realize that they represent goals you are working toward as a family. Success does not happen overnight. You need time, patience, and follow-through, and each of these resides in you.

After several mornings of following through with your plan of action, consider the changes, major and minor, your family has made. The improvements may be small at first, but they will be there. It may encourage you to keep working if you jot down some of the good changes you are witnessing from morning to morning.

Use this small morning diary to make some notes for yourself, and make sure to focus on what you do differently in response to your children's behavior. Remember that lasting change begins with you. When you start taking notes, begin with yourself and your behavior. Do not automatically begin to list the behaviors of your children in order to divert yourself from the task at hand—you. Focusing on your children prevents you from looking at what you might be doing to contribute to the chaos.

## Changes in My Morning Routine:

First day _____

_____

_____

_____

Second day _____

_____

_____

_____

Third day _____

_____

_____

_____

Fourth day _____

_____

_____

_____

Fifth day _____

_____

_____

_____

If you made a plan, changed your responses to your children's behavior, and followed through with consequences, then you will soon begin to see very definite and even dramatic changes within your family. These changes should give you courage to continue, as well as bolster your faith in this approach to interacting with your children. Better yet, you can now actually start enjoying your children and the many contributions they can make to a peaceful home life.

# But What About
the Weekends?

Okay, you are primed and ready for your mornings Monday through Friday. You know what you are going to do about school and work and all the tasks that have to be accomplished to get your family out the door and on the way. But what about the weekends?

How do you handle, for example, fighting with your children about going to church with you? Since it is an optional activity, unlike school, you may find your children put up a great deal of resistance to the idea of getting up early, having to dress, and going with you simply because you want them to.

Rather than insisting, fighting, or bribing them to go to church, you need to back off. Think about how to win their cooperation. The way you do this is by letting go of trying to coerce them. You may succeed with your efforts to control, but it will come at a great cost. Not only will they balk, dawdle, and grumble, they will also be surly and resentful during church, which is embarrassing and unpleasant for you.

That is the way they want you to feel so that you will give up in your quest to get them to church. Your children's health and safety are not at stake here, so why not experiment with a different way of dealing with this issue in your family.

In the past, you have yelled, begged, used guilt, and bribery (breakfast buffet after the service?) but these do not really work because you find yourself repeating this battle every Sunday. This proposal is going to sound so simple you may say it will never work. But try it. For just a few weeks, give up control. On Saturday night, ask your child to join you tomorrow at church. Tell him you would really like to have him go with you. Then,

Sunday morning, get yourself ready for church and leave. When you return, say nothing. Just go about your Sunday routine.

The next Saturday night, do it again. Be neutral, calm, and kind when you invite your child to join you. Then wait and see what happens. Do not ruin this experiment with any recriminations, bribes, or lectures. Just wait. Should the child be up and ready on Sunday morning, smile at him and say, "I am so glad you decided to come with me." Say nothing more. Do not make a big deal out of his finally deciding to go. Enjoy your time together and let it be.

Many parents have talked themselves into trying this deceptively simple approach, and it works. Why, when all other approaches have failed or have ended in hurt feelings, unpleasant outings, and weekly arguments? It works for these reasons:

- It is respectful of the child because he is left to make his own decisions about this optional activity.
- It is respectful to you, the parent, because you simply state what you want without attaching conditions or using threats or treats to manipulate your child into doing what you want him to do.
- You are giving your child the most wonderful message a parent can give: *I want to be with you. I enjoy your company. I want you to come to an important activity with me.*

## This Chapter in a Nutshell

- Parents need a concrete plan of action in order to change their morning routine with their children.

- Children need the knowledge and tools (such as alarm clocks) to begin taking responsibility for the simple tasks associated with the morning routine.
- It is all right to take a child to school "as is" if the child has chosen not to get completely dressed.
- Children can and should be involved in all the chores of the morning, whether it be putting out breakfast or cleaning up the dishes.
- There is far too much parental involvement in getting children up and ready for the day.
- Plan ahead for your morning routine by creating timelines that will help guide you out the door.
- Plan how you will handle sleeping in on the weekends.
- Try something new! Invite your child to go to church with you if that is what you like to do. Make your invitation with no strings attached so the child is truly free to decide whether to go.

# 5.

# Respect: What Does It Really Mean?

*"Kindness implies a genuine
respect for another individual.
It does not require
submission."*

—RUDOLF DREIKURS

Most of us agree with Dreikurs' statement. The irony is that even when they believe these words, many parents do not apply this maxim to their children. Why is it that when it comes to children we do not feel respect is important in the way we interact with them? Perhaps it is because of the way our parents treated us, or perhaps it is because we are the product of a "spare the rod, spoil the child" social philosophy.

Whatever the reason, it is important to begin to think about respect in terms of the way you respond to your children. Respect for self and for others is the foundation for all of the techniques this book addresses. In order to develop self-control, self-respect, and true respect for others, there are practical steps you can take to change yourself.

Here are some ideas to keep in mind:

# Idea One:
# The Golden Rule

In relationships we generally get back what we dish out. If we think we need to use power with our children, we will get power back from them. Respect is essential to the most fundamental ideas in this book, and not just respect for others, but respect for self as well. The whole idea that changing the relationship you have with your children begins with changing your responses is all about self-respect. A parent who yells, hits, or threatens in an attempt to control children is not a parent who enjoys self-respect. In fact, when you behave in these ways, you demonstrate that you are bankrupt of good ideas about how to handle the situation.

You need to understand that this type of reaction demonstrates a lack of self-control. It is as if the person who "loses it" is not even aware that there may be another way to handle the situation. The very *idea* that there should be self-control is absent, along with the behavior that would demonstrate it.

In addition, those who are on the receiving end of your acting out will not respect you. When you are ruled by your emotions or the crisis of the moment, you are not in control of your responses. We as adults do not like it when children are rude, loud, out of control, and throwing a tantrum. But this is exactly what you model when, as a parent, you do not control your emotional reactions to your children.

This lack of control leads to responses that may be inconsistent, extreme, and irrational. After an outburst where emotions get the best of you, you feel terrible. You have no self-respect, and you are aware that those who have observed your behavior (or been the recipients of it) do not respect it, either.

To let anger, frustration, or the need to control and dominate fuel your responses to your children (or to anyone) is to forego self-control, which, in turn, is to forego self-respect. We know all of these things when we consider our work environments or our adult social relationships. We may even carry through with these ideas as we deal with our spouses and the adults in our immediate families.

However, when it comes to children, all these ideas seem to fly out the window. Children have a way of pushing adult buttons. Powerful children know where your Achilles heel is, and they will use it. Why? Are they bad children? No. They have found an easy way of feeling significant through the use of power.

You must also realize that your behaviors have become predictable (as have theirs). This is all a game. The children know that no matter how loud you yell or how much you threaten, your overbearing behavior will only last so long. They also know that when the dust has settled, you will likely feel remorse and give in to whatever the conflict was about in the first place. Who would respect you after that?

A lack of self-control is also evident when, instead of "losing it," a parent bribes, cajoles, or gives in to a child's demands just to keep the peace. This parent finds it easier to placate and avoid the hard work needed to discipline effectively and teach the child how to behave. This is not respectful to either you or your children. Children know what is going on. They may not be able to verbalize what the dynamics are that occur between them and their parents. But when it is pointed out to them, they recognize it for what it is.

You can ask a three-year-old what it takes for him to wear his parents down and get what he wants. The child will tell you what he must do to get mom to cave in. Children do not think about these things in the same way that adults do, but they know what is happening and what works in their relationships with their parents.

Sadly, these parents, not knowing what else to do, continue to act like doormats.

To stop being pushed around by their children and to begin to achieve self-respect, parents must learn self-control. As has been pointed out before, to do this parents must give up trying to manage their children and focus on managing themselves. Here's how the process works:

(This process, modeled by parents, teaches children what respect is.)

Household anarchy

Desire for change

New parental responses

Self-control

Self-respect

Respect for children and others

In addition to learning to respect yourself, you also need to rethink the idea of respect for others and take into account the ways that you have been acting and reacting within your family. Simply put, how do you treat your children?

Treating children respectfully is not just about using a calm tone of voice or stopping punitive responses to their misbehaviors, though both of these are important. Respect is also not just about having good manners, although behaving politely is part of the whole package. Respect goes much deeper. It is an appreciation of the other person as an individual who is separate and apart from you.

This separate person has ideas, thoughts, and feelings that are as valuable and important as yours. He or she is also responsible for all their actions, just as you are. It is no help to our children when we get wrapped up emotionally in the things they should be taking responsibility for, and, in fact, it stifles and inhibits children's growth toward independence.

Modeling respect for your children includes how you treat your spouse in front of your children. Part of your new efforts to take responsibility for changing your reactions may need to be directed toward the way you treat your spouse. Children watch and know what is going on between mom and dad. They sense tension, conflict, disagreement, and disharmony even when parents may think they are hiding these things from them.

Some parents engage in open warfare in front of their children. Not only are they forgetting how hurtful and frightening this behavior is for their children to witness, they also lose sight of the fact that their children are learning to deal with others in ineffective, hurtful ways. Let's be brutally honest. When parents openly engage in put-downs and disrespectful behavior with each other and their children become upset, it is not good enough merely to say, "Don't worry. Things are okay." Children *do* worry. Your soothing words in the aftermath of a flare-up between you and your spouse do not matter. What matters is the behavior your children see and hear. No words make up for that.

It is not that you and your spouse will never have problems that you must find ways to resolve. Rather, it is that you must find new ways of going about it so that your children do not hear yelling, threats, or constant criticism between mom and dad while you are telling them things are "okay."

Parents need to communicate respectfully and settle their differences in private. Remember, this is a crucial step toward gaining self-control and self-respect. It is not all right to "let it fly" in front of your children. All you are teaching them is how to be disrespectful, and that is the last thing you want.

What should parents do when they experience sudden conflicts? The same principles hold true. Treat each other with civility and respect in front of the children. Discuss the issues calmly. Many times, issues should be discussed privately. Establish these ideas firmly in your own mind so you will be ready to implement them when conflicts arise.

One of the common areas of disagreement between parents is how to raise their children. One is typically a pushover or an easy mark and the other is tougher. Each parent thinks his or her way is the best. They compete with each other for the children's loyalty and continually criticize and blame the other in front of the children.

If you are truly concerned about the best interests of your children, even though you disagree with each other, you need to find ways to compromise and work together. Parents need to agree on one primary thing: that they will commit to improving things and learning what they need to form a parenting plan they can both endorse.

The problems that arise in this context are really marital problems disguised as parenting issues. They need to be addressed as such and not confused with your responses to your children's misbehaviors. It is easier to fight about the children than it is to address the resentment, competition, and power struggles between husband and wife. Consider: Are you modeling for your children power struggles between you and your spouse? Are you living in a constant state of resentment?

If you want to do something about your parenting but do not feel you can tackle marital issues that impinge on parenting, the next best thing to do is to take responsibility for your own discipline relationship with your children. It may be that when you change yourself, your spouse may notice the easier time you are having with the children. Your spouse may be encouraged to believe that change can occur and will follow your lead or want to know what you are doing that is working. And you may improve your relationship with your spouse by using the same techniques and attitudes that you are implementing with your children.

## Idea Two:
## It Takes Two to Tango

It is impossible to fight, argue, engage in power struggles, or attempt to dominate *when there is only one person engaged in the battle.* You are the adult, and it is up to you to control yourself and stay out of power struggles. But, you say, should I just let my child get away with bad behavior?

This is where your new philosophy about the children's mis-behavior and your responses to it come into play. If you choose to participate in the power struggle, you are responsible for half the problem. Your children cannot fight with you or try to wear you down if you do not engage with them.

For example, suppose you call your twelve-year-old daughter to dinner, and she ignores you because she is talking on the phone with a friend. In an irritated tone, she says, "Dad, please, can't you see I'm busy?"

If this dad is not careful and not in control of his reaction to his daughter's rudeness, he could find himself in a power strug-gle very quickly. He might become angry and say, "Get off the phone right now or I'm yanking that thing out of the wall." He could threaten her with dire punishments and restrictions if she does not get off the phone.

He might yell, curse, slam doors, or do any of a number of things that would indicate to the child that he has lost it. And guess what? If he does any of those things, he will not just lose his temper, he will lose the power struggle and his daughter's re-spect, to say nothing of his own self-respect.

If dad is committed to changing his behavior, he will not re-spond verbally or physically to her rudeness. Instead he will go about his business, eating dinner with the other members of the family. If the girl does not come in to eat, her dinner is put away without comment and she misses the meal.

If the daughter appears before dinner is over and sits down to eat, dad does not comment on her earlier rudeness, nor do other members of the family. They carry on as usual, eating and talking normally. Dad is thinking about consequences that would be logical for this situation.

Either way, he has avoided engaging in a power struggle with his daughter. He has recognized that fighting with her and responding in anger means he has lost his self-control. In order to respect himself, dad has decided not to do the usual thing. Since he did not engage in a screaming match, he feels better about how he handled himself. In addition, he has set the stage for implementing logical consequences in a respectful way.

The consequences for this kind of behavior on the child's part are:

- She gets no reaction from her dad.
- If she comes to the table late, she misses dinner.
- Dad may decide to remove the phone in her room for a period of time as a logical consequence.
- Dad may decide that this is behavior that calls for a statement from him concerning how he felt about her rude treatment of him (this talk should be done privately and in a calm moment).

When dad implements any or all of these logical consequences, a powerful child will escalate, trying once again to get a reaction and provoke the power struggle she is used to waging and winning. In order for dad to truly change his interactions with his daughter, he must be ready for the child to escalate the battle. He needs a plan so that he will not be drawn in and "lose his cool," which he knows will not work and is not good for him.

Here is what works. When the child sulks, throws a fit, accuses her parents of being cruel, or slams out of the room, dad adopts a neutral posture, looking befuddled by her behavior.

The reason he acts as if he's befuddled is because he does not understand what all the acting out is about.

She did *A*, for which the consequence was a logical *B*. The lesson has been taught. He has faith that his daughter "got it." And she did. There is no reason for dad to respond to the escalation.

Dad needs to remove himself, in a nonhostile way, from the scene of her tantrum. When the child gets no response, she will eventually stop her misbehavior. There is no one to fight with! What is more, she *knows* this all makes sense. She is the one who did something wrong, and she is the one who must face the consequences. And, believe it or not, she not only respects her dad for doing what is right, but she also feels respected because he did not attempt to control or dominate her through power, nor did he rescue her.

## Idea Three: Good Things Come to Those Who Wait

Children will often surprise you if you give them enough time. Unfortunately, most parents have a tendency to be micromanagers who try to control every situation. That is what all the yelling and/or placating is about in the first place.

Your child has misbehaved, and you feel you must handle it right away. You must jump in and take over, even though your child has defeated such efforts on your part time and time again.

If you are this type of parent, then you routinely take responsibility for your child's misbehavior, trying to fix things by punishing your child or by cajoling and bribing your way out of the conflict. Your assumption is that without you and your in-terference, your child cannot know what he or she has done wrong or how to make it right. When you assume your child is incapable of "getting it," you are disrespecting and insulting that child's intelligence.

What happens when parents decide to wait it out? Yes, as a rule you should implement consequences quickly when children misbehave. However, there may be times when it may be best to wait and see what the child does next. Your children may re-think their choices and decide to do as they have been asked. Or they may think about their misbehavior and come to their own conclusions about changing it.

You may decide to use this waiting option when you feel the child's misbehavior or rudeness is not a major transgression. For example, if all your child is doing is grumbling or procrastinat-ing, imposing consequences immediately may not be as effective as giving him the opportunity and time to think and then do something differently.

One example involves eight-year-old Chloe. Mom and dad are talking with her in the living room about wanting her to contribute by setting the table for dinner each night. She protests that she will miss her favorite television program and it is too hard to set the table. She storms out of the room in a huff. Mom and dad take a "wait and see" approach instead of fol-lowing her down the hall or yelling at her to "get back here."

Thirty minutes later, Chloe finds her mother in the kitchen and says, "I'm sorry I walked out when you were talking to me." Her mother hugs her and tells her that she is happy that Chloe has spoken to her about her misbehavior. Mom then continues on with what she is doing.

Mom and dad are wasting their breath if they try to explain

what just happened or reinforce the lesson that has been learned. The child knows what she did, and she has taken care of it. All that remains for you to do is accept her statement, recognize that she is taking responsibility and thank her (without praise). You might also show some faith in her by saying, "Now it would be a big help to me if you would set the table."

This mom has done something wonderful. She has changed her typical responses to Chloe's bursts of temper. Mom resisted the urge to lecture Chloe about how badly she behaved and the guilt the child should have felt after she was rude. Mom has not made a dark cloud appear over the kitchen in response to her daughter's rude behavior. This is truly respectful.

## Idea Four:
## Facing the Music

Earlier, we discussed the importance of allowing your children to face the consequences of their behavior and why it is disrespectful either to rescue them or control them through your parental power. What you need to do is become a neutral party who implements consequences instead of an arbitrary boss who dispenses punishment based on your emotional state at the time.

It is hard to stay emotionally uninvolved when your children are directly challenging you. Remember, they know you very well. They know what buttons to push. Your challenge is to exert the self-control needed to remain calm and teach what the child needs to learn. What will help you stay calm is your plan to respond differently and your commitment to what you want for your children for the long term.

What also will help you stay neutral is the realization that all your yelling and punitive actions, as well as your rescuing, have not brought about change in your children's behavior in the past. If those tactics were going to work, they would have worked a long time ago. You would not be experiencing these same conflicts over and over again.

Logical consequences take the place of these old tactics. It is not that you are doing nothing, it is that you are doing something different. For consequences to work, they have to make sense. They must be related to the misbehavior in some way. They also must be consistent and occur every time the misbehavior does. You must not slip back and forth between the old tactics and your new responses. Remaining neutral will help you stay in the new modes.

See yourself as a teacher, not an enforcer. The consequences are the lesson, not the punishment. When used with anger, perfectly good consequences become punitive, which leads to the child's rebellion. Your anger and outbursts now have made you a part of the problem.

It is important not to begin this new approach of responding unless you are convinced it is the right way and you believe you can and will stick to it. Otherwise, the children only learn that now it will take a bit longer to get a reaction from you. You will have created a worse problem than the one you had before. You must be consistent, firm, and kind every time in order for consequences to work.

It is hard to know how to get started changing your responses unless you have spent some time thinking about what your old tactics are. Do you yell and scream? Do you threaten dire punishment and then cave in? Do you swat? Do you use sarcasm? What are the behaviors you have used in the past that you now want to change? Look at the example below and think about what your old responses might have been.

*Six-year-old Hillary dawdles over her cereal in the morning and plays with the cat instead of eating. If she does not hurry up, she will make everybody late. What are some responses you might have had in the past?*

*I would say* _____

_____

*I would do* _____

_____

*I would feel* _____

_____

Now that you have isolated the "wrong" responses, list some things you will use to replace them.

*I will say* _____

_____

*I will do* _____

_____

*I will feel* _____

_____

The time to plan your responses and make sure you are up to implementing consequences is before the conflict, not during or after. If you do not do some work now to be ready for the misbehaviors that will occur in the future, you will not be able to make these changes.

You cannot be consistent when you are acting in the heat of the moment. You need to be prepared so that you are ready with new responses, not trying to think them up as you go.

If you get into a situation where you do not have a plan, say to the children, "I do not know what the consequence will be for this. I have to think about it." Give yourself the time to make a wise choice. This also models self-control.

Think carefully when choosing consequences to be sure they teach a lesson. For example, if your two sons are arguing in their bedroom after they know they should be in bed, ignore it and stay out of the way. That is one consequence.

Another is to separate them with as little talk as possible and have one boy sleep on the couch. The logic is that their behavior tells you that they have decided not to stay together, since they are doing what they know they are not supposed to do. You can make this connection for them or not. They will most likely get the point on their own, so you only need say it once, if at all. But is one of the boys getting the consequence while the other remains in his bedroom? Not really. The consequence is about the separation of the two, not about who has to sleep where.

Occasionally in implementing any consequence, siblings will be drawn in when they actually were not participating in the misbehavior. This is okay because you are teaching all the siblings, those who are misbehaving and those who are not, what happens when one misbehaves. Everybody sees what the limits are when consequences are implemented this way, and all the children learn about the impact of their behavior on others.

The parents in this example have resisted going in with a "Who started this?" mentality that would draw them into a power struggle with the boys. Give up the role of referee. It will get you nowhere but mired in an argument. Who started what is not the problem. They are cooperating in their misbehavior. Put them in the same boat and apply consequences to both. Just make sure the consequences fit the misbehavior.

Separating the boys makes sense here. It does not make

sense to storm into the room, demand silence, and tell them you will withhold their allowances for the next week if they do not go to sleep. They know (and so do you) that you will not follow through with that threat. And the threat itself makes no sense to anyone. It is not tied to the misbehavior.

As you remove one child, be sure not to talk other than to say something like, "You will sleep on the couch since the two of you decided not to be together." Your demeanor should be firm, kind, and neutral. At this point, one of the children will want a second chance.

As you know, in order to be consistent and follow through with consequences when you make them, you must not give second chances. This defeats the purpose of the consequence and tells your children they can wiggle out of taking responsibility if they are contrite.

Second chances lower their respect for you because you have gone back on what you said. Go ahead and enact the consequence, but also demonstrate faith by letting them know that you are sure that they will do the right thing tomorrow.

## Idea Five:
## Think Before You Act

When you are confronted with your child's misbehavior, you have three ways to go. You have old, ineffective modes of responding such as yelling, threatening, spanking, or "losing it." Or you can choose another old way, which is trying to placate, bribe, whine yourself, cater, give in, buckle, become a doormat. Or you can remain neutral.

Remaining neutral is always the best choice when your children are challenging you. It is comforting to know that when you are faced with the same old misbehaviors from your children, you will now have something completely different to do in response.

Let's say you are fully committed to the idea of taking a neutral position, implementing logical consequences, and adopting new responses in order to teach your children better ways to behave. Neutrality occurs when the adult looks at the child with a bit of confusion and says very little. It is important to explore this idea of neutrality and fully understand how to use it in order to be successful with this key response.

Do not confuse neutrality with lack of interest or simply not caring about what your children do. The reverse is true. Your neutrality is a response chosen for specific reasons, the primary one being that it is respectful and keeps you out of the fray. You remain calm and polite while you consider the situation and think before you act.

The worst thing a parent can do is react to a situation without thought. This may be what your children are used to. In the past, you have been caught up in the misbehavior. You have responded in the heat of the moment, not with careful thought. Now you are ready to do it differently.

But merely being calm and polite is not enough, though it is essential to true, respectful neutrality. Consider this:

*Seven-year-old Sean takes a bath, but stays in the tub playing long past his bedtime. He will not get out of the tub and into his pajamas, although his parents have asked him two or three times to dry off and get to bed.*

*Mom decides she will try something new. She comes to the bathroom door, arms folded across her chest, unsmil-*

*ing, and stiff-backed. She looks at Sean and, in a very calm, polite voice, says, "You have a choice. Either you get out of the tub and into bed or I will take you out and help you into your pajamas." She then raises an eyebrow, taps her foot against the floor, and gives him a cold, hard stare, waiting for his defiance.*

What is wrong with this picture? Mom thinks she is being neutral because she is not screaming. Her words are good and delivered in a calm tone. But mom has blown it. She is giving many signals that tell Sean she is not neutral at all. Her body language, facial expressions, and tapping foot tell him he is getting to her, as always, even though she is not yelling at him. With her nonverbal cues, she is engaging in the power struggle even though she thinks that by controlling her tone she is doing the right thing.

The point to remember about adopting neutrality is that it will not ring true unless you commit to it 100 percent. Your body language, expression, tone of voice, and physical movements must all match your words in order for this response to be effective. Fall down in just one area, and you have not controlled your response. Instead, you have failed to resist the urge to let that emotion out. Your consequence-implementing process is seriously undercut by such a lapse.

There are going to be times when you will be angry, irritated, or hurt when you are dealing with your children. There is no denying that you will have strong emotional feelings about things. The key to respectful discipline is to remain neutral during the consequences phase. But when you are calm and the moment is right later on, you may take the opportunity to talk with your child about the effects of her behavior on you.

Do not act out of anger or frustration. Talk about it with your children. There is a big difference between demonstrating your anger in the heat of the moment and talking about your anger later after everyone has calmed down.

You are not being asked to be an automaton. The neutral approach is not a response without feeling. However, it is an approach that asks you to control your feelings and deal with them later at a better time.

It also asks you to determine which misbehaviors you need to address in a conversation with a child and which can just be handled with consequences alone. The more serious issues may need to be discussed, but you will not be able to do an effective job of talking if you are trying to do it when emotions are high and tempers are at work.

Yes, it can become very difficult to maintain neutrality when your children escalate after the consequence. They may beg, say mean things to you, scream, threaten, slam around the house, or do any number of things to provoke confrontation. Your emotions may be challenged. That is their purpose in goading you.

Do not fall for it. Instead, recognize that you must exert control over yourself in order to stop the escalation. You can adopt a pleasant, somewhat befuddled demeanor and, without hostility, remove yourself from the scene, suddenly remembering you have a chore to attend to in some other location.

Nonverbal cues are just as important as your tone and words in any relationship you have. We all know when we are being sarcastic or saying one thing when we mean another. Children can read us, too. They know the voice might sound nice but the daggers coming from the eyes counteract what is being said.

Your body language and facial expressions convey messages that are sometimes even more powerful than the words you say.

Be aware of how you look and what postures you use when you are disciplining your children. You do not want to give them mixed messages.

# Idea Six:
# Cultivate the Quiet

Talk is cheap, and it can be highly overrated as a means of good parenting. Talk, used incorrectly, is just another tool of control, interference, and manipulation. It is lazy parenting to rely on talk instead of taking the harder route, which requires thoughtful action.

Rudolf Dreikurs observed that, "Talking is one of the most ineffective things to do." You can probably think of times when you talked a subject into the ground with no results. Never tell a child what he already knows. That is disrespectful and assumes a lack of intelligence. But adults continuously repeat themselves over and over to children.

The less you say, the more power your words have. Good teachers know this. When you are quiet, your children want to know what you think. When you do speak, they listen more attentively to what you have to say. Try it. Let them *ask* you what you are thinking instead of *telling* them all the time.

In our culture, as a rule, parents feel that if they do not talk, they have not taught anything. They do not believe their actions carry weight. And even when they have taken the right action, they feel they must reinforce it with their kids by using words, words, words. They want to drive the point home over and over again.

Be honest. You have probably said, more than once, something like, "I'm not just saying this to hear myself talk," or, "Are you listening to me?" We have already discussed the great importance of thinking before you act, but now consider that perhaps it would be of great help to your family if you also think before you speak.

Two things may happen when you speak without thinking. First, you may say some pretty hurtful and damaging things that it will be hard to rescind later. Even when you apologize, painful words tend to linger. Second, your words may be insincere or false. In this case, your children know that you do not mean what you say, so their respect for you is damaged. Your words lack credibility.

We seldom get it right when we act or speak without thinking. The counting to ten rule before speaking is always a good device to gain some time before saying or doing something you might regret.

# Idea Seven:
## What Really Matters

"A child should be commended for what he has done, not for what he is, be it nice, handsome, pretty, or cute." This statement from Dr. Dreikurs tells us to look at behavior rather than at the superficial qualities of the individual.

Children learn very early that they may get away with certain bad behaviors if they are cute, charming, sweet, et cetera. But these are not good life lessons to learn, and your job as a parent is to teach something else. Teach your child that actions, good behaviors, thoughtfulness, caring, contribution, and cooperation carry more weight than physical attributes or charm.

Also, you need to separate the "deed" from the "doer." When you do this, you enable yourself to keep all the good feelings you have about your children even when they misbehave. You get to love, enjoy, and value them even if they are not always acting the way you want them to. The feeling that the children get from this type of parental attitude is one of unconditional love for them as people.

The child knows his parents are able to separate his worth from his sometimes-bad behavior. It is this ability to value the child even when the behavior is bad that lets the child know his parents ultimately believe in him and lets him know he is capable of being better.

All of these things are part of the bedrock of respect that is so essential to family relationships. And a key part of maintaining this respect and this valuing of each child is to avoid scrupulously comparing one sibling to the other. If one child excels in school, that is great. But that child is not any more valuable or important than the child who struggles.

The "old school" of parenting taught that you should hold back love and esteem in order to motivate your children. The love and esteem would be the rewards given to those children who succeeded. If you were raised this way, with a carrot-and-stick mentality, and the carrot was your parents' approval, then you know how terrible it feels when you do not quite make it and the carrot is forever out of reach.

This is a technique of manipulation that we now know does not work and, in fact, is very bad for your relationship with your children. The focus needs to be on your children's characters, including efforts that they show, special gifts they have, empathy for others, and unique qualities that make them who they are.

You may have a child who does not excel in school but is creative, interested in many things, and extremely loving to all members of the family. Yet you may focus only on the thing he does not do well. What a terrible disservice to this child.

Instead of looking at your child's shortcomings, try to stop for a moment and think of each child's individual gifts and abilities. What sets each of your children apart from the others? Enjoy these special qualities. Let your children know you appreciate these things they each have and that you love them for their uniqueness.

Why not build on these strengths instead of trying to squeeze all children into the same mold? What is stopping you? Is your need to control getting in the way of your appreciation of your children? If it is, that is the cornerstone of your difficulties in your relationship with them.

It is the lazy parents who criticize and nitpick endlessly, never pleased by anything their children do. Or, if they are pleased by something, it never occurs to them to draw the child's attention to his strengths and how highly his parents regard him for them.

There is a saying that "all a child needs is one adult who thinks that he is the greatest thing since sliced bread." Think what this might have meant to you as a child. If you did have one such person in your life, think of the difference it made for you. It is a small thing to do for a child, yet it is so important and meaningful. Who better to do it than a parent?

Unfortunately, parents have gotten sidetracked on this issue. Many of them feel that it is their job to criticize and correct. In many cases, pointing out the negative becomes the only means of communication between parent and child. What a message these children are getting!

Now is the time to change this attitude and this direction in parenting. Get rid of it. Make a list of each child's shining attributes be they ever so humble. You will see your children in a whole new light. And let them know you do. This type of encouragement will result in less misbehavior.

If you have any doubts that this attitude is effective in improving your relationships with your children, try it out. Take a week and offer no criticism or correction whatsoever. Notice what the child does that is positive and comment only on those things without lavish praise. See the effects this small change has in just a week.

## Idea Eight:
## Tomorrow Is a Day Away

The final, and perhaps most important, aspect of showing true respect for your children is to have faith in their abilities and willingness to do the right thing. A key point made by Dr. Dreikurs is that, "Faith is the basis of encouragement; to believe in others, not merely in their possibilities, but in them as they are."

This is a fundamental appreciation of another person's character. It is your acceptance of that individual as someone who, at heart, wants to do the right thing even though he or she may not always succeed. We seldom have a problem extending this kind of acceptance to our adult friends. Why, then, is it so difficult to think this well of our children?

Some parents even go so far as to adopt the belief that a particular child is "out to get me." If you really believe the worst about your children, you will get the worst. They pick up on these types of attitudes and do one of two things.

They either pay their parents back for the low opinion they hold by acting out just as expected, or they take it out on themselves, believing they are bad. They fail in school, use drugs, get pregnant, and do a host of other self-destructive things.

Instead of seeing the child's behavior as their trying to "get" you, see it as a bid for belonging and importance. This is something you can address and change by your reactions. Your child is not a "bad seed." When you believe the worst, there is no way out, no hope for change in your relationship with the child.

Where is your faith? Where is your optimism? See their bad behavior for what it is and do not take it personally. Otherwise, you are going to say and do things that will alienate and discourage your children. This is the last thing you want to do.

Once you take it personally you have lost the ability to control your emotions and actions. You have limited your ability to influence the child positively. Giving up on your child is the worst thing you can do. Allowing yourself to feel hopeless is an indulgence that parents simply cannot afford.

If you are able to implement this new approach with your "worst" child, you will find that one of your other little darlings will often move into the recently abandoned "bad child" niche. This happens because children are competitive with their siblings and because they believe there is only one place in the family for a good child.

The "good" child feels displaced and quickly moves into the available slot. This should demonstrate to you that misbehavior is all about belonging and jockeying for significance, not about "bad seed" children who are just made that way.

Realizing this is very eye-opening and encouraging for parents. It means you can make a difference. It also means your children are not incorrigible. Now your challenge is to eliminate the competition in your marriage and among siblings. You do it by using all the eight modes of showing respect discussed in this chapter.

Parents must not be guilty of having low expectations for their children. Think better of them than that. Have high expectations that they can do many great things. Let them know you believe they can improve, get organized, make contributions to the family, help others, cooperate and feel important every day. Why not expect the best?

Another word of caution about the most important thing to consider: You must be ready to start this process and you must commit yourself fully to it. If you waver, backtrack, or make mistakes as you implement these changes, you will create a worse situation than you have now. What you do to get back on track is acknowledge your mistakes to yourself and your children and restate your commitment to work for change. Then get right back up on that bicycle and start pedaling!

# This Chapter
# in a Nutshell

- Self-control and self-respect go hand in hand. Parents who are committed to making positive changes in the family dynamic must gain self-control in order to change their responses to their children's misbehaviors. This leads to self-respect when emotions are mastered and empty threats are no longer the major means of communication between parents and children.

- Change must first begin within the parent. Change your attitudes and behaviors if you want to change your children's misbehaviors.
- Respect is important to every member of the family. The youngest child is deserving of and wants respect. Respecting your children means waiting to see what they will do rather than micromanaging and overtalking.
- Instead of criticizing and focusing on the children's weaknesses, try noticing their efforts, special strengths, and unique abilities.
- Demonstrate faith in your children, even when they are misbehaving. Always say, "Maybe it will go better next time."
- Have high expectations that your children will "get it" when you implement consequences. Believe that your children can and will learn the lessons you are teaching them.
- Think before you speak and act. To be in control of your emotions is to be able to form a plan so that you are acting instead of merely reacting to your children's misbehaviors.
- Take action instead of talking so much.

# 6.

---

# Still Have Questions? What to Do When . . .

*"One does not win the friendship and regard of a child by humiliating him or by giving in to his whims."*

—RUDOLF DREIKURS

Could it possibly be true that you are getting something out of your family dramas and crises? Think carefully and honestly about whether or not you are gaining your feelings of importance by making your children needlessly dependent on you.

When you nag, cajole, lecture, browbeat, and micromanage, you are telling your children they cannot do the simplest things without you. You feel needed, important, and secure in your knowledge that you are the center of their universe. You are a good parent, right?

Wrong. Your feelings of security in your parental role are

really false feelings of importance based on the dependency of those around you. These are not relationships of equality and respect.

This may also be the case for the relationships between many spouses, too. Living this way is a very subtle power struggle that has as its goal to weaken the other party and make that person need you. Only through their dependence do you feel secure.

You may also be finding importance by getting attention when you talk about how awful your children are. Your friends and family may give you all the sympathy and empathy you could ever wish for when you are lamenting your terrible situation with those children on whom you lavish such good care. If kids hear you making these kinds of statements, they will repay you in spades. Look at your own psychological needs that motivate you to downgrade your children to others. Take responsibility for your role in the "bad" situation in which you live.

It is important to come to terms with what motivates your behavior. At the beginning of this book, the emphasis was on creating positive change by first changing your own behavior. Unless you understand what your behavior is, where it comes from, and why it is not working, you will not be successful in trying to change it.

In this chapter, the focus will be on how to be consistent, follow through with consequences even in the face of your child's escalation, and stick to it when the going gets rough. You will not be perfect as you put this new process into place in your family. You will "fall off the wagon" along the way. We all make mistakes. The question is not can we avoid making mistakes? Rather, it is what do we do once we make them?

First, you must admit you made a mistake, and you must let

your children know that you did something incorrectly and that now you must do it again another way. Say, "I blew it yesterday when I _____. From now on, I am going to be more respectful and do _____."

As has been said before, you must also come up with some plans of action to help you refine your responses so that you are not trying to change things in the middle of a conflict when emotions are high. That is why this chapter pays particular attention to planning responses to various kinds of conflicts and the escalation children are likely to use when the parents do not respond the ways they have in the past.

The most important thing to remember is that you are not going to punish your children anymore. Instead, you are going to remain neutral in the face of your children's misbehaviors and escalations, and you are going to implement logical consequences that have a connection to the misbehavior. You are going to refrain from overtalking about these new responses and simply have faith in your children's intelligence and ability to understand.

With these things in mind, let's discuss the allowances that you give your children. Most parents still follow this practice and give each child a set amount of spending money. A child's allowance is a natural weapon for parents who are intent on punishing. "I'm taking away your allowance for a month!" is a common threat. It is also usually an empty threat because children need to buy many things such as school supplies and the same parent who confiscates an allowance may find himself, once in a better mood, buying the necessary items for the child himself.

This is not to say that a child's allowance may not figure into the logical consequences a parent may implement. For example, if a child is responsible for certain chores around the house and does not do them, a typical parental response might be to yell, nag, and take away the child's allowance.

In implementing a logical consequence when the child does not do his chores, instead of nagging and complaining, the parent says nothing. In fact, mom simply does the chores herself without comment.

On allowance day, however, she deducts money to "pay" herself for doing his chores for him. When the child says, "Hey, you didn't give me all my allowance," mom may calmly say, "Yes, that is right. I washed the dishes twice this week, so I paid myself. I deducted the cost of my doing your work." Then mom goes about her business, no further explanations needed. She has followed through with a consequence that has a direct application to the misbehavior, and she has not engaged in any kind of power struggle over how or when the chores get done.

This mom has not only made her own life more pleasant by resisting the urge to engage in a fight with her child over the chores, she has also taught a very good and valuable lesson. If the child escalates, demanding his full allowance or promising that next time he'll do better if she gives him the whole amount now, she simply goes about her business, surprised and a little puzzled about his escalation. He had chores to do. He did not do them. Someone else had to do them for him. That other person should be compensated. It seems pretty simple to mom, so she does not feel the need to explain or talk about it.

The only response mom should make to any of this is to show faith by saying something like, "Maybe next week things will go better." Other than that, she is done. The lesson has been taught, and, regardless of how her child escalates, the lesson has been learned. When you disengage, your child wants to goad you into the response he is used to. That is why he escalates. If he can get you going, he has a chance to bully you into giving him his whole allowance.

If, like the mom above, you walk away and refuse to play this game, you make several points:

- You will pay yourself out of his allowance each time you must assume the responsibility of his chores.
- You will not engage in any kind of argument or escalation that will allow him to indulge in a power struggle.
- You have faith that he will do better.
- You are in control of your responses and cannot be goaded into a fight.

Parents generally feel tremendous relief when they are no longer fighting about things such as chores. It takes enormous energy and creates anxiety and emotional turmoil to fight over things such as whether or not your child took out the garbage or fed the dog.

It is so much easier on parents who have worked out a plan of action and created some options for implementing consequences so that they can remain calm when the child escalates. Think about some of the arguments you and your spouse may have had with your children in the past. Have there been times when you started out with a seemingly innocent request or question and then found yourself embroiled in a full-scale fight over something insignificant? That is what happens when you engage in a power struggle of any kind with your children. Added to that, you may find yourself in an escalating argument with your spouse about how you handled the situation.

There is nothing like self-control to provide you with a feel-

ing of well-being in the eye of the storm. Yes, at the time it might be easier and even feel good to "let fly" and purge your emotions by yelling, threatening, or punishing. But in the long run, you are just making yourself feel worse, as well as perpetuating a cycle of disrespect your children will observe and imitate.

The following charts show strategies for changing your responses by implementing logical consequences.

| Misbehavior | Your Response | Escalation | Your Response |
|---|---|---|---|
| Children do not come to the table when called. | Remove their plates and put dinner away. Say nothing. | Children demand snack food, say they are hungry, throw tantrums. | Remove yourself from the conflict. Go to another room. Do not engage. Carry on with your evening as usual. |

*Observations:*
- You may also take the food you have prepared and put it in the freezer, give it to the neighbors, or deliver it to a local soup kitchen. The point is to make the meal unavailable once the children have chosen not to eat it. Use these responses for whatever misbehaviors your children exhibit at mealtime. They work when your children are fighting at the table, talking back, whining, or complaining about the food.
- You need to be firm, consistent, and kind. Do not cave in when your children are contrite. Do not offer more food until the next meal is served. You are doing the right thing, and your children will not be harmed by missing one meal.

| Misbehavior | Your Response | Escalation | Your Response |
|---|---|---|---|
| Child walks out the door to the car but balks because he wants his "special cap." The family is late. The child whines beside the car and will not get in. | You give the child a choice, "Would you like to get in on your own or would you like me to help you in?" The child does not move, so you help him into the car. | Once in his car seat, the child begins to throw a tantrum, demanding that you go back and get his cap. | You do not pay any attention to the tantrum. You do not go get the cap, nor do you talk about it or try to make him feel better. You drive on as if nothing were happening. |

*Observations:*
- An alternative to keep in mind when kids misbehave in a car is to announce just once that you cannot drive with all this racket, and pull over and wait. This is especially effective when you are going to an event of theirs.
- Be aware a child uses misbehaviors like this in order to manipulate parents. Do not take his hysterics and drama at face value.

| Misbehavior | Your Response | Escalation | Your Response |
|---|---|---|---|
| Children are late getting out of bed. They become mesmerized by the television and are not getting dressed for school. | You say nothing. You simply turn off the television set and go about your business. They are supposed to get ready, and they know it. | The kids become furious and start yelling because their favorite cartoon was on. | You take the neutral position of befuddlement. What is all the uproar about? You turned off the set because it was in the way of them getting ready for school. |

Observations:
- Neutrality works especially well when children have escalated a power struggle to wear you down and get what they want.
- The children know they should get ready and that you are leaving at seven-thirty. You do not need to impose another consequence for the yelling. Neutrality is enough of a consequence and it keeps you out of arguments.
- When you are neutral and return to getting ready yourself, the children have no one to argue with. They may just get ready.

| *Misbehavior* | *Your Response* | *Escalation* | *Your Response* |
|---|---|---|---|
| It is bath time, and your child refuses to get in the tub. | You say, "That is your choice, but you cannot go to the birthday party tomorrow after school unless you are clean." | He yells and screams that it is not fair and that his friends do not care if he comes to the party without a bath. | You remain neutral but firm. Do not take him to the party even if the next day he changes his mind and decides to bathe. |

*Observations:*

- Once a consequence is enacted, there are no second chances. You may express faith that next time he will want to bathe.
- If the child is old enough, you may want to stand back and let him go to school and the party without bathing. His peers and siblings will take care of it for you because they will probably tease him unmercifully.
- Be prepared at party time for a major meltdown. Do nothing other than remove yourself from the scene of the drama.

| *Misbehavior* | *Your Response* | *Escalation* | *Your Response* |
|---|---|---|---|
| The kids are squabbling at the table during dinner. | You ignore their behavior. | They get louder, more physical, spilling milk and upsetting plates. | You should take your plate and go to the patio and eat without saying anything. |

*Observations:*

- Nine times out of ten, your children will be upset that you have left the room. They will feel bad because they want to be with you, even when they are giving you trouble. They are sensitive to your perceptions of them and will try to get back in your good graces. They may come and apologize.
- The message you are giving is that the children have a right to squabble, but you have a right to eat in peace and will leave the room to do so.
- Removing yourself is an alternative to removing them or removing the food. Any of these three consequences will work.

| *Misbehavior* | *Your Response* | *Escalation* | *Your Response* |
|---|---|---|---|
| Child is rude to waitress in restaurant and will not choose a menu item. | Ignore the child's behavior. Apologize to the waitress. Leave the restaurant saying, "I see you have decided that we should go." | Child tells you he is sorry and promises to be good if you can go back inside the restaurant and eat. He is very contrite. | Continue on home. There are no second chances. If you say anything it should be something like, "We will see how it goes next week." |

*Observations:*

- Any misbehavior in a public place means the family leaves. If you wish, you can take two cars on an outing so that one parent can leave with the misbehaving child while the rest of the family continues the event. You can let the child know it is his choice to leave, but other than that, you say nothing. You should show faith in your child by indicating that next week you will all try again.

- Do not "overtalk" and lecture, telling the child, "You see what happens when you misbehave? The whole family has to leave." The child gets the message without hearing about it from you. You do not need to say anything. In fact, if you lecture, you divert the child from processing what has happened and learning the lesson you have just taught. The focus becomes your talking instead of the child having time to think about what happened.

| Misbehavior | Your Response | Escalation | Your Response |
|---|---|---|---|
| Child dawdles and does not get dressed. When it is time to leave, she is not ready for school. | Take the child to school as is. If you talk, say, "I see you have chosen to go to school in pajamas." | Child starts to cry and get upset about leaving in pajamas. She refuses to go to the car. | Do not engage in the temper tantrum. Calmly give the child the choice of walking to the car on her own or being carried there by you. Carry her to the car if need be. |

*Observations:*

- You will most likely only have to implement this consequence one time. Your child will probably not want to repeat her misbehavior because she is no doubt going to be embarrassed by arriving at school in pajamas or in some other stage of unreadiness. Your child needs to leave the house on time, ready or not. The consequence is that she goes to school in pajamas. That is the lesson.
- You may allow her to take her clothes with her so that she can change at school if you feel too squeamish about this consequence. The point will still be taken. Again, you need not explain or lecture about this process. The child gets it. You should also express your belief that "things will go better tomorrow morning."

| Misbehavior | Your Response | Escalation | Your Response |
|---|---|---|---|
| Child refuses to sleep in his own bed. He gets up over and over each evening. | Once he has had his routine drink of water, bedtime story, and bathroom visit before bed, that is enough. Say nothing. Take the child back to his room every time he gets up. Then go about your business. | Child cries loudly. He screams that he's afraid of the dark and you are cruel to him. He will not get into his bed. He comes to your door and demands to sleep in your bed. | You may need to lock your door once or twice. If he cries outside your door, ignore him. He may fall asleep on the floor. Cover him with a blanket if necessary, but let him sleep there (or anywhere else in the house). |

*Observations:*

- You thwart your child's independence every time you cave in and let the child keep getting up out of bed or allow him to sleep with you. Sleeping in his own bed is important to building independence and taking care of himself.
- Your child will not be harmed by spending one or two nights sleeping on the floor of his room or in some other part of the house. When you let him sleep where he chooses, you are teaching him that you will not engage in power struggles. Nor will you let his tears manipulate you into caving in. These are all part of the consequences he experiences when he does not sleep in his own bed.

| Misbehavior | Your Response | Escalation | Your Response |
|---|---|---|---|
| Child will not leave television program to get ready for bed even though it is the appointed time. | Without comment, you turn the television set off and go about your business. | Child complains loudly and turns the television set back on when you leave the room. | Physically remove the television from the room or disable it if need be. Continue your routine. Expect that the child will get ready for bed. |

Observations:

- A powerful child will defy you, trying to draw you into a confrontation and wear you down so that you will give in. Your refusal to be drawn in is one of the consequences he experiences. He is unable to engage you in an argument that is meant to exhaust you until he gets his way.
- By turning off the television set or removing it from the room, you deal with the problem immediately rather than being diverted by the confrontation you normally would have had with your child. You have demonstrated self-control by refusing to engage with him and by saying nothing in the face of his escalation of misbehavior.
- The child learns that he cannot get the results he expects by escalating the argument. He may abandon the misbehavior and go to bed as he should.

| *Misbehavior* | *Your Response* | *Escalation* | *Your Response* |
|---|---|---|---|
| Child will not do homework and wants to talk on the phone to her friends instead. She knows she is supposed to have her schoolwork done before bedtime. | You say nothing. When her bedtime comes, you may say, "I see you have chosen not to do your homework. Now it is time for bed." | Child cries and begs to stay up an extra hour. You are a terrible mother. She will get in trouble if she goes to school without her homework. She has to do it now! | Adopt a neutral stance and remove yourself from the conflict. Do not respond to the homework issue. |

*Observations:*

- There is nothing to fight about. The child knows she needs to have her homework done before bedtime. She has made her choice.
- This is a perfect time to act befuddled by her behavior. When she tells you what a terrible mother you are and how she will get in trouble at school, you simply look confused by the whole concept. It was her choice not to do the homework, so you do not know why she is so upset about it now.
- No matter how much you would like to say this, do not. You need not say a word. The child knows. Your silence is respectful and shows self-control.
- The phone can be removed for a time as it was the "thing" that interfered with the homework.

| *Misbehavior* | *Your Response* | *Escalation* | *Your Response* |
|---|---|---|---|
| Children will not stop bickering and fighting. They are supposed to be making their lunches for tomorrow, but they are accomplishing nothing. | Put away all the lunch things without comment. Say, "I see you have chosen not to take lunches to school tomorrow." Go about your business. | Children tell you they are sorry and they will stop fighting and make their lunches now. | Do not back down by giving them second chances. Missing one meal will not harm them. Do not buckle and give them lunch money. |

*Observations:*
- This is one of the toughest consequences to follow. However, the lesson is an important one. The children need to learn to take care of themselves by taking on and completing their responsibilities.
- This is a logical consequence that will most likely be implemented once. Children learn quickly and do not repeat the behaviors. They also learn about respecting each other and not fighting.
- You have a right to a peaceful evening that does not include listening to your children fight with each other. They need to cooperate and meet their responsibilities. Perhaps they thought if they fought, you would make the lunches just to have a little peace. This consequence teaches many lessons.

It is important here, too, to discuss some issues that surround cooperation and contribution. Contribution is a means of providing children with positive opportunities to belong to the family and gain importance. It is an antidote to all misbehavior.

But when you have children, especially older children, for whom this is a brand new idea, you are going to need patience to bring changes about.

Remember that you are dismantling a system that may have become very comfortable and familiar to your family. Doing things differently does not occur overnight, but it will occur. You must give your children time to absorb different ways of doing things, as well as time to learn the lessons you are now teaching as you implement consequences and alter your responses.

The key to succeeding over time as you begin to implement consequences and watch for changes in everyone's behavior is to have faith that your children can learn, change, gain independence, and gain importance, in the best sense of the word, through contributions to the family. There are so many ways that your children can contribute. First of all, children need to learn that just by taking care of themselves they are making a tremendous contribution to the family. When your children clean their rooms, put their clothes away, keep their toys picked up, get up on time, brush their teeth, put on their own pajamas, go to sleep, and do all the other things a person must do throughout the day without your having to orchestrate these actions, the whole family benefits.

There is no longer any need to fight, throw temper tantrums, manipulate, or engage in power struggles. Everybody in the family has more time, more peace and quiet, and more opportunities to like and enjoy each other. This is cooperation, and that is, perhaps, one of the most important contributions a child can make.

In addition to taking care of themselves, children may also make contributions by taking on household chores, pet care duties, and meal planning and cooking. When everybody is pitching in, the workload is much lighter. But beware. Are you the kind of parent who gets an emotional payoff by having to "do everything so it gets done the right way"? If you suspect you might be a martyr to your family, you need first to address your own issues and change your own responses to your family's efforts to help out.

Is it possible that you have actually been discouraging cooperation and contribution because it takes away from your "good" parenting? These are some things to think about as you begin to work toward household harmony. You may have to give up some misbehaviors of your own (like perfectionism!).

Encourage your children to take on tasks. This is the easy part of implementing a routine of contribution and cooperation. Now comes the difficult part. You must step back and give them time to do whatever it is they are supposed to do. For example, if you have all agreed that little Joey will take the trash out, you need to let him do it. Perhaps he will have a timetable of his own that says trash will be taken out just before he goes to bed. However, in your mind the trash needs to go out right after the kitchen has been cleaned up after dinner.

In your haste to get this chore done, you may look around, notice that the trash has not yet been taken out and immediately pounce on Joey, nagging him and insisting that he take the trash out now. You may then feel the need to lecture him on not doing what he agreed to do. It probably never crosses your mind that if you had just waited, he might have taken the trash out without any problem.

Remember those high expectations? Now's the time for you to have them in abundance. You need to believe that your children will do their chores, and, most of the time, they will. Showing respect for your children means letting them make some

choices about when they will do the chores rather than imposing your timetable on them. Elicit their preferences about when
they will take out the trash.

You may go to the living room, slip your shoes off, and relax. Isn't this preferable to hovering over your children to make
sure they do what they are supposed to do? It is certainly more
relaxing for you. You might grab quite a few minutes of reading
or television watching for yourself, or you may be able to spend
some enjoyable time with your spouse, if you will just back off
and trust that your children can and will do what they are supposed to do without your interference (verbal or otherwise).


## Eating, Sleeping, and Getting Up Contributions Children Can Make to the Family

- create menus
- make grocery lists
- help with meal preparation (for example, make salads, cut
  up vegetables, pour water, put bread on a plate, set out
  condiments, actually cook the meal as they get older)
- help younger children choose clothes to wear to school
- help younger children get dressed in the morning
- make lunches for the whole family
- do the dishes and help straighten up the kitchen after meals
- help other children do their homework
- make their beds and help younger siblings with this task
- fix after-school snacks for everyone (peanut butter on apple
  slices, for example)

- read or tell bedtime stories to other children (kids can rotate this duty)
- take mom or dad the paper in the morning
- lay out breakfast items
- help younger children set their alarm clocks
- take out the trash
- sweep the kitchen floor
- help mom cook some extra meals for the freezer on the weekends
- get up early to get ready for school so there will not be a log-jam in the bathroom
- help siblings order at a restaurant
- accompany parents to the grocery store and help get all the needed items (without asking for special treats or whining)
- help unload and put away groceries
- clean out the tub after bathing
- help prepare a special dessert

This is by no means a complete list. You will probably be able to think of a great many more things your children can do to contribute to the family. Sit down with your children to draw up your own list of contributions. Get their input. You might be very surprised by what they have to say.

Ask them which things they would like to do and encourage them to look on this as an adventure in doing things differently and learning to appreciate each other. Do you doubt that your children need structure, peace and quiet, cooperation, and respect any less than you do? You shouldn't.

You may even draw up lists of chores and see who volunteers to do what around the house and for each other. This will be an interesting exercise for you and your children to get to know each other and cooperate in making a plan that everyone "buys into." This will be much more effective than you telling the children what to do. There is no reason these lessons cannot be fun.

You can even make some of these things into games (but not games where children are bribed or rewarded). The games you might use could be everyone writing chores on slips of paper and putting them in a jar. Then each child draws however many slips you have all agreed on, and each child will be responsible for the chores he selects. You may rotate the chores to let everyone have a chance to learn to do all the daily tasks.

Once you and your children have agreed on some chores they can do and some contributions they can make, you might think you are well on your way. However, be prepared with a plan or two for the times your children "fall off the wagon." Children may readily agree to do all these things you discuss with them, but when the time arrives to do them, they may balk or refuse. Now you must be ready with good logical consequences that teach lessons so that you do not fall back on your tired, old behaviors of yelling, punishing, threatening, or bribing.

Remember to expect great things from your children and let them know you believe they can and will do the chores they select. Do not praise them lavishly, though, for doing things they should be doing in the first place. Hollow praise is insincere, and your children will wonder why taking out the garbage is so praiseworthy. It will sound as if you expect so little that even the tiniest action on their parts is cause for celebration. That is pretty insulting if you stop to think about it.

Once this process begins, though, there will be times when you will need to implement consequences when the children misbehave over contribution issues. Here are some situations and plans of action to guide you as you teach your children about contribution.

| Misbehavior | Your Response | Escalation | Your Response |
|---|---|---|---|
| Child is supposed to set the table for dinner but is upstairs playing with toys and does not come down and complete her chore. | You set the table and "pay" yourself out of the child's allowance. Or you could simply sit down and stay there, telling the hungry family, "I cannot start dinner until the table is set." | Siblings complain to child and she finally comes down and sets the table so you will cook the meal, but she sulks throughout dinner and plays with her food. | Remove her food, saying, "I see you have chosen not to eat your food." Say nothing else as everyone continues on with dinner. If she leaves the table, do not follow her. |

*Observations:*
- The trick is to be ready with logical consequences for both the misbehavior and the escalation. You need to remain in control of your emotions and not "lose it" just when you have the opportunity to teach the lesson.
- Many times, your best response to misbehavior is simply to stop what you are doing and sit down. Simply say, "I cannot cook when the breakfast dishes are still in the sink," or something of that nature. You need no further explanation. Everybody needs to take care of their responsibilities if the family is to eat.
- When you get the opportunity, let the child know you have faith that tomorrow evening will go better. There is always another opportunity for success.
- One mother served the food right onto the table since there were no plates. This made quite an impression. Do the unexpected sometimes.

| Misbehavior | Your Response | Escalation | Your Response |
|---|---|---|---|
| You have asked the family to help get yard work done before you all go out for your weekly dinner at a nice restaurant. Everybody helps but one son. | You announce that this boy will be staying at home with a sitter whom he will pay out of his allowance. | Your son complains loudly and makes excuses for why he didn't work. | You ignore. Do not involve yourself in any discussion. The family leaves after the sitter arrives. |

*Observations:*
- It would be wise to have a private discussion later with the child who did not work just before he goes to bed. Let him know how you felt when he did not help the family.
- This process is followed without ridicule or "rubbing it in" to the boy left at home. Train your other children to be matter-of-fact. Your son made a choice so he is now living with it.

| Misbehavior | Your Response | Escalation | Your Response |
|---|---|---|---|
| Child is supposed to do the dinner dishes but instead goes up to his room to play video games. He goes to bed without doing his job. | Mom may do the dishes and "pay" herself out of the child's allowance. Or she may just leave the mess, say nothing, and continue on with her evening. | The next morning the child has a fit because he needs to get to the soccer field early for practice and mom is just sitting in the kitchen reading a book when he comes down for breakfast. | Mom calmly says she cannot make breakfast or leave on time because the kitchen is such a mess. She has the morning off. |

*Observations:*
- Mom does the "sit down" routine in order to implement consequences. She is under no obligation to bustle around doing her son's chores so he can get to soccer.
- Mom remains neutral and, if anything, slightly confused about her son's distress. He has not done his chore and she has enacted the consequence. Enough said.
- Missing soccer practice or breakfast will not harm the child. Even if he hops-to and does the dishes, mom should not take him to soccer. Remember, no second chances when children suddenly realize their misbehavior will affect them. That is the point. The child must experience consequences in order for the lesson to be an effective one.

The blank grid that follows is your map for planning your new set of responses to your childrens' misbehaviors. Give careful thought to how you will act and speak when these misbehaviors crop up again. Write your own script and rehearse it so you are ready to practice these new responses.

| Misbehavior | Your Response | Escalation | Your Response |
| --- | --- | --- | --- |
|  |  |  |  |

Observations:
- 
- 
- 
-

You may want to copy this grid and draft several plans for each child and each set of misbehaviors that you might encounter. The only way you will succeed in changing your behavior is to create some new responses to use in place of what you have done before. You may want to make two separate grids, one showing the responses you do now that you want to change, and one showing the responses you will use in the future.

You will want to consider many other applications for the techniques discussed in this book. These methods work for any discipline situation. They work for all kinds of relationships. You will find them useful for dealing with friends, family, and coworkers, as well as other people's children. Once you've mastered the basic techniques, brainstorm some creative ways to deal with stress and conflict in other relationships and situations.

But remember that it is very important to get these ideas clear in your mind before you begin putting them into practice. Know where you are going and what you are trying to achieve. Be creative. The examples given here are suggestions, but you may have some unique and interesting applications that will work very well with your family. The only caveat is that you must be kind, firm, respectful, and you must follow through with consequences.

Another thing you can do to help you succeed with your plans is to tell other people what you are doing and ask for their assistance. For example, if it is your intention to take your children to school "as is" for a few mornings so they will experience the consequences of dawdling, you may wish to talk to their teachers and school administrators.

Your intention is not to cause trouble for your children at

school. You simply want to enact consequences so that they can learn. That is why it is helpful to inform people who will come into contact with your children about what you are doing and why. You may also want to share your plans with other family members (grandmothers, aunts, uncles, and so on) so that they, too, understand what is going on.

You are doing something important for your family. Telling people about it may also help you be strong when the tough times come along. You may need to enlist some support for the changes you plan to make in yourself, too. It is not easy to go it alone, and friends and family may have many valuable observations to contribute as you begin to evaluate your self-control and self-respect issues in order to change your attitudes and responses.

If you are committed to giving these techniques a try, prepare as best you can and go for it! There is no time like right now for giving your children these valuable learning experiences. Good people do not just spring out of nowhere. It takes loving teachers to guide and train them. How fortunate for your children that you have decided that a parent's greatest role is that of teacher. You will never regret the time and effort spent showing your children how to live well in the world.

## This Chapter in a Nutshell

- You must fully commit yourself to doing the hard work needed to begin changing your responses and changing your children's misbehaviors. These are not easy things to do.

- Honesty is essential for parents to practice when they have committed to doing this work. If you slip and revert back to old behavior or do the wrong thing, you need to be honest with yourself and with your children and let them know.

- The logical consequences you implement should relate to the misbehavior. If you are not careful when you choose consequences, you may find yourself falling back on your old patterns of empty threats or outlandish punishments that come "out of the blue."

- It is important to plan what you will do and say when your children misbehave. If you do not have a plan in mind, you may give in to the heat of the moment and "lose it."

- You must try for calmness, neutrality, and respect every time you respond to your children's misbehaviors. You are modeling the very important concept of self-control for them.

- Be ready with more than one set of responses for each misbehavior. Remember that your children will most likely try to escalate the conflict. They are trying to wear you down until you cave in and let them do whatever it is they want to do.

- Plan, plan, plan so that you can think before you speak and act. If you feel you are on the verge of an emotional outburst or a wrong response, tell your children you must think about some consequences and you will get back to them once you have done so. Then remove yourself from the conflict.

• Every time you exercise self-control and respond in a calm way to your children's misbehaviors, you are lowering your stress level and increasing their respect for you (not to mention what you are doing for your own self-respect).

# 7.

# Some Afterthoughts on the Quality of Life

*"Most people get exactly what they want—only they don't know that they want it."*

—RUDOLF DREIKURS

This book opened with the radical idea that if parents are truly interested in changing their children's behavior they should first look to their own attitudes, beliefs, and patterns of doing things. Change first begins within each parent.

The three arenas of conflict are eating, sleeping, and getting up, and the focus has been on how you can change your responses and implement consequences that will change these former battlegrounds to areas of cooperation and contribution that benefit everyone in the family.

But in this "afterthoughts" section, there is an opportunity to devote some space to broader issues that touch on ways adults can go about making life-altering changes in patterns that may have existed for years. Planning ahead is always a good first step for any project, and it is doubly important when you are contemplating changes that will affect your children, your spouse, and perhaps other members of your immediate family.

In order to come up with some planning techniques that will assist you, the focus will be on the three designated areas of conflict and the "quality of life" issues you may need to address before you are able to begin this important work. First, give some thought to how you define an elusive idea like "quality of life."

## Quality of Life

"A good quality of life" is the phrase that most often pops up when we are asked what we value. But what is it really? Where we live? How we live? With whom we live? What things we possess? How smart or pretty or successful we and our family members might be?

When we say "quality of life," we are generally not talking about material possessions. Quality of life is that elusive but overriding idea about what things we think are most important. And, like other nonmaterial things, definitions of "quality of life" are dependent on the values and beliefs of each family.

A way to begin thinking about how you define "quality of life" is to make a list of the things you believe are the most important to you. This is your list to help you prioritize and learn about yourself, and it should not reflect anyone else's attitudes or wishes. Just for this moment, be purely selfish and focus on yourself.

Having a good quality of life means bringing those things that are important to you into the forefront of your consciousness and working to maintain them. You may find that your list is at odds with the life you are currently leading.

Most of us are not living exactly as we would wish, but many people are much closer to their ideal than others. That tells us that it is possible to live differently and have a better quality of life.

The list you are drawing up will give you some ideas about setting goals for change within your family. For example, one of the things on your list might be that you believe sharing more family time together will improve the quality of your life, but the reality is that you and your children and spouse rarely see one another with all the activity in your household.

It is a worthy goal to set for yourself to incorporate more shared time with your family into your life. If you do not articulate the ideal, you will never be able to move in that direction. Once you have drawn up your list, think about how it relates to your life as it actually is. What things are you doing that are in opposition to what you really want?

For instance, if what you really think you need in order to improve your quality of life is peace and quiet, yet your list shows that you are engaged in power struggles and conflicts that have you yelling and fighting with your children, you can instantly see that something must change in order for you to enjoy what you want. But what must change? The easy answer is, "Well, others must change and give me the peace and quiet I want."

The harder answer is, "What am I doing that prevents me from having what I want in my life?" In other words, if you truly want peace and quiet, why are you yelling and fighting? You need to analyze carefully what you want when you are faced with a gap between what you say you want and what you do. It cannot all be someone else's fault. You are contributing to your situation in some way. Perhaps there is a payoff for you that you have never even considered consciously.

For example, perhaps your parents waged war with each other or with you and your siblings. Unconsciously, each time you wage war with members of your own family, you may be repeating patterns that feel familiar. Your unconscious payoff is that you are going along experiencing business as usual, which, for some reason, feels right even though you know in your conscious mind that it is all wrong.

One of the most important things you can do as you create your wish list of how things should be is to consider what you are getting out of the way things are. You must be willing to give up these "payoffs." True change shakes us to our foundations and makes us question everything we do and search for better ways.

There is a certain amount of discomfort to be endured as we give up habitual behaviors that have some distant meaning for us that we have never confronted before. But be honest. That is exactly what your family needs if you are caught up in cycles of conflict that are destroying your relationships.

Your mission to achieve a better quality of life consists of some simple steps to help you get started:

- Define what you mean by quality of life.
- Name the things you would like to have in your life that you do not have right now.
- Look carefully at the discrepancies between what you want versus what you actually have.
- Analyze why these discrepancies exist. (Do not blame others.)
- Be brutally honest about your contributions to the chaos and conflict in your family.

- Look for payoffs you might be getting from your current behavior patterns.
- Make a plan for changing your behaviors in order to improve your life.

It is not enough to just think about these things. An architect creating a bridge cannot think up the idea in his head and then construct the whole thing without a physical blueprint. Your plans need to be written down and revised as many times as necessary in order to come up with the one that is going to work for you.

You have a unique opportunity to craft the world you would like to live in, if only on paper at first. That is the first step toward realization of your goals.

This is even something you may wish to do with your children later after you have done the work on your own. Help them be the builders of their own blueprints for life. Ask them to draw up plans for changing things and improving the family's quality of life.

This could be a very enjoyable evening activity for you and your children. What do you think they would have to say about all this? It will certainly be interesting to find out, because quality of life means something different to almost everyone. Your children may be quite young, but they will already have formed many opinions on what things they would enjoy in their lives. You cannot hope to have an improved quality of life unless you can first define it within your family. Start now with this exercise:

*To me, quality of life means*

_____

_____

_____
_____

*To improve my quality of life I need*

_____
_____
_____
_____
_____

*To get what I need for my improved quality of life I will*

_____
_____
_____
_____
_____
_____
_____
_____

## Some Thoughts to Ponder About Eating

Misbehaviors surrounding eating and mealtimes have been discussed through the use of many typical examples. But there are some other things to consider as you come to terms with this topic.

Spend some time thinking about what you do when it comes to family meals. For example, what are your family's patterns of eating, and what is your contribution to the pattern.

It seems lately that many parents have been caught up in buying fast food. Some parents rely on it to the extent that their families exist on a nutritional treadmill of breakfast snacks on the run, fast food lunches, and more trips to different fast food restaurants for dinners.

Somehow, people have gotten the mistaken idea that there is no time to prepare food to eat at home. In addition to spending too much money eating this way, families who are going non-stop morning until night, now add another activity to the roster by driving from one quick, unhealthy meal to the next.

If this does not make you nuts, nothing will. It seems some families who protest there is no time to fix good meals will spend an hour or more going to a fast-food place to eat tasteless and nutritionally harmful or depleted food that they must order, wait for, and consume in a hurry.

With just minimal preparation ahead of time, that same hour could be spent in your own kitchen with everybody pitching in to make a delicious, nutritious meal that everyone enjoys. It takes minutes to make a salad, heat up an entrée that you have made ahead of time, and put out some bread. And it is far more cost-effective.

In addition, you have scores of opportunities to teach your children basic life skills when you are all working together to prepare a meal. You certainly do not have those opportunities if you stop at a fast food place every night. There you are teaching your children how to ignore their health and well-being.

If you want to have warm, shared family times and great opportunities to get to know your children better and improve your relationships with them, you may need to rethink the way your family eats. If members of the family are too busy for meals at home, or if you feel you have no time for anything but fast food, you need to sit down and really think about your priorities. Is it more important for the children to eat bad food really fast because they are late getting home due to some activity or is it more important that they get home early and spend some enjoyable time with the whole family getting a meal together and sharing it?

Something simple such as getting your family off the fast food circuit can make a big change in how you all relate and learn to enjoy being together. How? Here are some simple ways to start rethinking mealtimes in your family:

- Make a commitment to curtail the fast food stops.
- Stop snacking as a means of meal replacement (for example, do not grab a pastry on the way out the door in the morning and call it breakfast).
- Once each week, create a series of menus for meals (this is a great one for your children to help with).
- Do some of your cooking on the weekend and freeze meals that can be quickly reheated for dinners (instead of one meatloaf, make two and freeze one).
- Make a decision that everybody will begin taking lunches from home for school and work (what a money-saving idea this is!).
- Pack and refrigerate sandwiches, fruit, yogurt, and things of this nature for lunch the night before so that they are ready to grab as you head out the door.
- Have everybody take responsibility for making their lunches each night, or rotate this duty so that everybody takes a crack at making the family's lunches throughout the week.
- Buy fruit or raw vegetables to replace fatty, salty snack foods.

- Rotate cooking and prep duties so that everybody gets to do something different throughout the week.
- Keep plenty of cereals, whole-grain frozen waffles, low-fat milk, juice, and fruit on hand for breakfast. (It takes less time for everyone to eat a bowl of cereal, juice, and fruit each morning than to go to a drive-through, order, and eat on the way to school.)
- Plan, plan, plan—to free yourself and provide more time for relaxation and enjoyment of your family, you need to get organized, especially with meal preparation and eating.

The whole point of changing what, where, and how you eat is that if you are a frazzled wreck at the end of the day, it may be that you need to slow down and begin taking control of some of the things that have you running around needlessly. Planning and executing meals is one place to begin the quest to cease all the driving and start enjoying some family time.

When you draw up menus to prepare at home, they need not be fancy, just wholesome and healthy. It is not difficult or expensive to prepare food this way. There are cookbooks by the bushel-basket out there for people who want to put together good meals in a short amount of time. Invest in one for you and your family to use. It will be a great adventure to begin choosing menus and cooking together.

And remember an important lesson you are teaching your children when you take the time to put together good meals: There should always be time to take care of yourself. You need to schedule yourself into your days, and it is important that your children know this, too. If you do not, then you are telling your children that everything else you do is more important than caring for yourself. And that message is wrong.

## Some Thoughts About Sleeping

You probably do not get enough sleep. Most people do not. But have you ever thought about why this might be the case? Oh, yes, we are all too busy. But who says we are too busy to sleep? Where does this idea come from?

Now is the time to think about what it is that keeps you from sleeping. Is your evening routine so chaotic that once you finally get the children to bed you are so distressed that you literally cannot get to sleep? When you are stressed and feeling anxious, and the adrenaline is pumping because you have been fighting with your spouse or children, you most certainly will not sleep well or long enough.

But planning your evenings so that they go more smoothly is essential to changing things so that you can get to bed on time and get enough sleep. It begins with making sure that television does not interfere with all the evening's activities, either for your children or for you.

Do you or your children turn the set on the minute you come in? Do you get sidetracked watching some interesting program and let the minutes tick by until dinner is an hour late and everybody is behind in homework, getting ready for bed, readying backpacks and lunches for tomorrow morning?

Have you been so involved in your children's after-school activities that you get home late and have to scramble around to get things done? Are there chores and responsibilities you constantly "back burner" until finally they stack up and you must do them before you go to bed?

What can you do to organize your evening's activities so that you can get to bed and get ample sleep? Consider some of these options:

- Cut back the number of activities your children are involved in. (They may be just as relieved as you to have some down-time in the evenings.)
- Do not turn the television set on as soon as you get home to "watch the news" (and do not use watching the news as an excuse to stay up late and keep watching).
- Create an orderly plan with your children for how you will all work together to eat, clean up, do homework, choose outfits to wear in the morning, make lunches, bathe, and get ready for bed.
- Recognize that for your plan to be effective, you need to schedule ample time to accomplish all these things—a half hour will not cut it!
- Restrict your family's television watching to the evening time after dinner, homework, and preparation for the next morning have been completed.
- Make some special time to talk one-on-one with each of your children before they go to sleep.
- Schedule your children's bedtimes appropriately so that they are not staying up late and demanding your time and attention when you need to relax.
- Schedule a time to get yourself into bed, just as you have scheduled times for your children.
- Keep to your schedule so that you get enough sleep.
- Do not distract yourself with magazines or projects that do not need to interfere with your evening.
- Do some yoga or some deep-breathing exercises that will help

relax you and get you ready to sleep. (Check books on relaxation out of the library and follow some of their techniques.)

- Enjoy your evenings rather than looking at them as some sort of punishment.
- Change your attitude about the evenings and make them work for you by helping the children pick out clothes for tomorrow, chatting about school while you make lunches, and reading the bedtime story while the kids are in the bathtub.
- Streamline your evenings so that you are doing what needs to be done, not a hundred little unnecessary projects and diversions.
- Take charge of what you do and how you react so that you help everybody have productive, fun evenings.

You can put organized, pleasant, helpful nighttime routines into place with just a bit of thought and planning. Let your children draft their plans for evening, too. Have them try to figure how much time it takes to actually do homework, pick out clothes for the morning, make lunches, prepare and eat dinner—all the things you and they need to accomplish.

You will all be surprised when you start tallying up the minutes you need to do everything, but this is how plans that really work get made. You must have a realistic idea about what you have to do and the time it takes to do it all.

And do not forget that it can be a lot of fun to sit down with your children and do this together. Furthermore, your children, since they have contributed to the planning, have an investment in making it all work. After all, they are the budding architects who are helping build your family's evening activities. They can be proud of this contribution to the family, and they will learn a great deal about cooperation as they put the plan into action.

## New Attitudes About Getting Up

It is our societal norm to have trouble getting out of bed, usually because we have been watching some old movie or late-night talk show on television into the wee hours of the morning. When the weekend comes, our collective desire is for one thing only: to sleep in.

Part of the problem, as mentioned before, is too little sleep, but another issue might be the dread many people have of facing another morning of conflict followed by a full day of work. Sleep is a wonderful way to avoid facing the day. Snuggling back down for a few extra minutes is an enticing thought, but the truth is that every time you do this, you contribute to the chaos of your morning and the disorganization of your day. Think about your morning routine as it now is and ask yourself some of these hard questions:

- Do I give myself enough time in the morning for all I must do? (Just getting up earlier would relieve so much of the stress and strain of the mornings for most people. If you are getting up an hour before you have to leave the house, you probably have not really thought about all the things you must accomplish and figured out how much time each task takes. You probably need at least another half hour or more.)
- Do I get up or do I lie in bed wishing for just a few more minutes in bed? (Getting up is not something you have to

like. You also do not have to think about it. You just have to do it. The minute the alarm goes off, get up—if you need to employ some of the techniques you are using to train your children, like putting the alarm clock on the other side of the room, then do so.)

- Do I need an attitude adjustment when I get up in the morning? (You decide what you are going to think and how you are going to feel when you get up in the morning. Maybe it is time to break some old thought patterns. Are you a person who snarls, "Don't talk to me before I have my coffee," every morning? Try doing something different. Be happy and bright before you have coffee. You might have to fake it the first few days, but after that you will find yourself actually feeling happy and bright. You can change your attitude and you will be surprised what an effect this has on your children.)

- Could I do some things each evening to make my mornings run more smoothly? (Live on the edge! Set the breakfast table the night before! Get your children to help you lay out everything nonperishable that is needed for breakfast. Put the coffee and water in the coffeemaker so that all you have to do in the morning is turn the machine on. There are so many things you and your children can do to create a pleasant morning for everybody. Why not try some of these things or huddle with your family and think up all the things each of you could do to make mornings better.)

- Do I practice self-discipline? It is just plain unfair to ask your children to behave in ways that you, yourself, are not willing to behave. You are also going to benefit greatly in terms of your self-confidence and self-respect when you do things that require discipline on your part. You will feel more in control of yourself and of your day, and you will not need to divert your energy in trying to control others. This alone practically guarantees reduced stress!)

The point of thinking about these things and choosing some of them to implement in your own life is that good quality of life is not an accident, nor is it a by-product of having lots of time or money to use to enhance your life. You must plan and organize to have the kind of life you want. And you must do some work to achieve the results you want. This work begins with you.

Something as simple as getting up forty-five minutes earlier and facing the day with a new attitude can have a huge impact on the quality of your morning and thus your whole day. You may be skeptical about some of these ideas, and that is fine. Not every idea works for every person. But try some of them. See whether or not some small changes reap large rewards.

If you are unhappy with some of the conflicts that are happening in your family right now, you have nothing to lose in working to replace those stressful moments with more positive interactions. The best part of this process is that you, the parent, grow and learn and change in positive ways. You are no longer stuck in ruts of personal behaviors and attitudes that you may have felt you could do nothing about.

Once you accept that you can change many things that you do not like about your life, you need to write down some of the things you will do to bring change about. Again, give yourself ample time to work on yourself and to see some results. These changes do not happen overnight. Try a few things over, say, a week or a month, and note what happens, not just with your family, but also within you.

If you change for the better, your family will notice and appreciate what you are accomplishing. You may even find that you have changed the whole tone of family interactions just by changing the way you do things and the way you respond to others. This is an exciting experiment, and you are the master technician who is going to get the whole process started! It is like planning a huge surprise for the people you love. And when you take time to think of things you would like to do and make plans to actually do them, you are making yourself happy, feeling more in control of your life, and adjusting your old attitudes to fit the new changes you are anticipating.

## Getting It All Together

Everything in this book comes under the heading of suggestion, and that is because it is really your choice to make changes in your own life and in your responses to your children. Nobody should be autocratic with you and tell you what you must do to improve the quality of your life.

The techniques outlined in these chapters *do* work, and they can bring dramatic changes to families in conflict. However, the key to really using these suggestions is to examine and understand your own family's dynamics. Families are like snowflakes, no two alike. That is a blessing and a curse when it comes to making changes. A book like this can help you by providing new ideas and different approaches to getting organized and improving your interactions with your children. But the truth is that you know the situation you are living in far better than anyone else.

Problems arise when we, as individuals, turn away from the task of examining our own behaviors, attitudes, and wishes. We sometimes do this because we have been taught that our needs come after everyone else's. Sometimes it is because the chaos of our personal feelings and attitudes seems insurmountable and we are afraid of what we will see when we closely examine ourselves. Perhaps you have avoided looking closely at your situation with an eye to change because it all seems so overwhelming that you do not know where to start.

Do not be afraid of this process. What you find when you look closely at yourself is what any human being will find. You are a mix of wonderful qualities and qualities that need to change. It is not a question of you being a good or a bad person. Remember earlier when we discussed separating a child's bad behavior from your overall feelings about the child? Well, you need to have the same care and concern when you examine your own behaviors.

Do not beat yourself up about what you perceive to be bad or negative things about yourself. Instead, look at these things as behaviors that you can change or eliminate from your repertoire. What a powerful thing it is to know that we can make these kinds of changes within ourselves. It means that we can create our lives regardless of what we have been used to in the past.

George Eliot, the great nineteenth-century author, wrote, "It is never too late to be what you might have been." What a thrilling thought this is. And this goes to the heart of questions you may have about the quality of your life and your interactions with your family members.

- What is it you want?
- How would you like to behave in your interactions with others?

- How will changing the quality of your life benefit your family?
- What do you need to do in order to have better relationships?
- Where does peace and quiet fit in your scheme of things?
- How do you teach your children (and maybe yourself) to appreciate the natural world and all the interesting and beautiful things that are in it?
- How does the lack of time and money become an excuse to stay on the treadmill and forsake your goal of improving your life?

It is never too late to change old patterns, adopt new attitudes, have the family life you want, and be happy with the life you have created for yourself. You will feel so much better about your life once you make some decisions about making changes.

And why not look at change as a challenge rather than a chore? There is something exhilarating about all the possibilities that open up to you when you embrace change instead of fearing it.

There is so much in life that is out of your control. Why not control what you can and relish the task? You may never have experienced the power and freedom of thinking about your life as clay that can be molded and shaped the way you want it to be. What do you have to lose when you replace old attitudes with new ways of looking at the world?

Just because you are so busy that you feel as though you cannot come up for air is no excuse to stay below the surface. You only live once, and you only have your children at home with you for a short time. Make the most of it.

Your stress level will go down because you are seeking ways to slow down and enjoy your children before they are grown and you cannot say where the time went. And, perhaps for the first time in a long time, you are thinking about yourself in positive ways. Here are some practice grids to help you formulate a plan for positive change in your life.

| Mealtimes at My House | What I Do Now | What I Would Like to Do | What I Can Change |
|---|---|---|---|
| We all eat at different times because nobody gets home at the same time. We grab fast food or something frozen and stick it in the oven so everybody can help themselves later. We do not spend much time together in the evenings, and we rarely talk. We are all too busy. | I do not cook even though I do enjoy it. I spend a lot of time driving my kids around. I feel guilty about the lack of nutrition my family is getting. I also feel like my children are growing up very fast and I sometimes do not think I know who they are anymore. | Sit down at least three times a week and share a meal with my children. Talk with my children about positive things instead of always nagging them about doing more or trying to get them to hurry up to get ready for this event or that lesson. I would like to be more rested. | I can schedule a family dinner three nights each week. I can help my children rearrange or pare down their schedules to be free and at home on these evenings. I can have my children help plan menus, shop, and cook meals so we have time to talk and share during these times. I can slow down and pay more attention to my children. |

Once you have made some lists such as this one, map out how and when you will implement some of these changes. For example, give yourself a two-week period to implement these changes and then make some notes on what happens over this period of time.

*I implemented these changes on* _____

*Observations on first week:*
- My children were reluctant to give up any activities. I had some doubts about whether or not this would work, but I persisted and asked each child to choose just one or two things to do in the evenings so that we could all have some family time together. They grumbled, but I did not respond to that. They did pare their schedules down.
- We had some difficulties with everybody in the kitchen at once. We talked it over and decided that I would be in the kitchen for the whole meal prep and cook time, but that the kids could come in and do their parts in shifts so we would not be so crowded.
- We all got together and created a rotating schedule for who would do what for each time the family has an evening meal together. There was some arguing about this part of the process, but I did not engage. By ignoring the arguments, I was able to let the children work out their schedules. I was genuinely surprised that they took it so seriously and did a good job dividing up the duties.

*Observations on second week:*
- We are falling into a pleasant routine. There is still some complaining and some requests for a trip to the fast food place for burgers, but it has almost become a joke among us all now. I do not respond to the complaining. We are making progress.
- I get an opportunity to talk with each of my children individually. I have found out many things about their activities at school, their friends, and the things they are interested in. We

are all more respectful of each other, although this is all new to us and we lapse into old behavior now and then.

- I feel I am doing a better job as a parent, not just by responding differently to my kids, but also because I am giving them good, home-cooked food that I know is nutritious. Also, I am talking with them about all kinds of things, not just, "Did you do this? Did you finish that? Why haven't you . . . ?" I feel our family communication is improving.

Now it is your turn. Use the blank grids that follow to make some plans for changes you would like to make. Make copies so that you can plan and execute many changes. Keep working and remember, progress may be slow, but it will occur.

| Mealtimes at My House | What I Do Now | What I Would Like to Do | What I Can Change |
| --- | --- | --- | --- |
|  |  |  |  |

*I implemented these changes on* _____

*Observations on first week:*

- 

- 

- 

-

*Observations on second week:*

- 

- 

- 

-

# This Chapter
# in a Nutshell

You can have the quality of life you want, and it is not dependent on more money or more time. You can organize and reprioritize your life so that you make space for all the good things that enrich you and your family. What is more, you can all grow closer. When you ask them to help you in daily tasks, they will learn to share, cooperate, and contribute.

This is the paradox of taking charge of yourself: Your life can be fuller, richer, more meaningful and yet slower, cheaper, and less filled with superficial activities. Not only is this better for you, it is better for your children. The benefits of changing your quality of life are limitless. You are embarking on a great journey of awareness. Take your children along for the ride.

# Sources

Adler, Alfred. *What Life Should Mean to You.* Boston: Little, Brown and Company, 1931.

Dinkmeyer, Don, and Rudolf Dreikurs. *Encouraging Children to Learn.* Philadelphia: Taylor and Francis, 2000.

Dreikurs, Rudolf. *Fundamentals of Adlerian Psychology.* Chicago: Adler School of Professional Psychology, 1995.

———*The Challenge of Parenthood.* New York: Penguin, 1992.

———*Social Equality: The Challenge of Today.* Chicago: Contemporary Books, Inc., 2000.

Dreikurs, Rudolf, Pearl Cassel, and David Kehoe. *Discipline Without Tears.* New York: Penguin, 1998.

Dreikurs, Rudolf, and Loren Grey. *Logical Consequences: A New Approach to Discipline.* New York: Penguin, 1992.

Dreikurs, Rudolf, Bernice Bronia Grunwald, and Floy Pepper. *Maintaining Sanity in the Classroom.* Philadelphia: Taylor and Francis, 1998.

Ricker, Audrey, and Carolyn Crowder. *Backtalk: Four Steps to Ending Rude Behavior in Your Kids.* New York: Simon & Schuster, Fireside Books, 1998.

Ricker, Audrey, and Carolyn Crowder. *Whining: Three Steps to Stopping It Before the Tears and Tantrums Start.* New York: Simon & Schuster, Fireside Books, 2000.

Schoenaker, Theo, and Eva Dreikurs Ferguson. *Dreikurs Sayings.* Cambridge, England: ICASSI, 2000.